Such Simple Elegance . . .

and the Best Part of It Is
I Did It Myself,
and It Is a Piece of Cake!

We Can Do It;
I'd Like to Share the Way.

Flying across the Pacific Ocean,
I am greeted with smiling faces on both shores.

How fortunate for an artist to be raised and nourished by an
ancient culture and its people with so much to offer,

and to be appreciated and developed by a young culture and
its people who show so much enthusiasm to receive.

Art knows neither time nor boundaries.

Chinese Brush Painting:
An Instructional Guide
by
Ning Yeh
for
Coast Community College District
Costa Mesa, California

Silk Era Corporation
Huntington Beach, California

David A. Brownell, Chancellor
Coast Community College District

William M. Vega, President
Coastline Community College

Leslie N. Purdy, Director
Alternative Learning Systems

David P. Stone, Assistant Dean

Mickey Jackson, Instructional Designer

Michael S. Werthman, Publications Editor

Judith Lindow McDuff, Assistant Publications Editor

Cover photo by Prasad

Published as the study guide for the telecourse
Chinese Brush Painting, with Ning Yeh
Second printing 1988

Preface

Who Is This Manual For?

Ever since I was seven years old, the practice of Chinese brush painting has been a constant source of joy in my life. As I grow older, the joy has been strengthened by a feeling of pride. Through the practice of painting, I feel a bond with the glorious civilization which generations of my ancestors built. Additionally, I see how relevant Chinese art is to the Chinese way of life.

From the time when I first started to read, I have been unable to resist any treatises on brush painting. I like to find out different methods to paint. I like to learn about the spirits, the stories, the romances, the poems and literature of the different subjects I paint. I like to hear from the artists whom I admire — their experiences and thoughts on their artistic pursuits.

In my own quest for answers to my endless interest in this topic, I have come across countless material, from the simplest to the most elaborate, from the most innocent to the most profound. When I found myself staying up all night to work on this manual, the question for whom this manual is written became very clear. "It is obviously for myself." This manual is, first of all, for me and nuts like me who never have had enough of Chinese brush painting.

This manual is written for beginners who never have held a brush before, for those who never have had any art training. However, I do intend to cover enough information so that artists at different levels might find this manual helpful. I do have faith in the everlasting enchanting facets of Chinese brush painting. Beware: Through this manual, a simple wish of "I would like to paint a bird for my daughter" can easily be turned into "I would like to become the founder of a Chinese brush painting society in my community."

This manual is written, not only for students of Chinese brush painting, but for those who are watching the series and want to know more about the telecourse.

In addition, I wrote this manual for artists of other media and disciplines, who welcome a different viewpoint and approach. For all the Chinese brush painters who wish to share their knowledge and skill, I hope this proven method of teaching can be helpful.

There are many different ways to do brush painting, and I hope the users of this manual can keep an open mind. I intend not only to train viewers to practice brush painting but also to appreciate brush painting in various schools and styles.

A Morale Booster

"My Dad is great, and modest too." — Evan Yeh

I used a computer to do this manual, and I am grateful for my son Evan's help in setting up this program for me. As he completed his assignment, I asked him to start a sentence for me. "Like what?" He asked. Just to boost my own morale, I casually suggested something like "My dad is great." I got the above statement instead.

I am the fourth-generation brush painter in my family, and there is no shortage of artistic ego in the long line of the Yeh family tradition. When I was Evan's age, I had ample occasions of having been coached to say "my father is great," but there was never a footnote such as Evan's. What we have here is a bit of the Americanization of the Yeh family. Such a transition, perhaps, is the cornerstone for this manual.

I have been intimately involved with brush painting for over thirty years. As a youngster growing up in Taiwan, I was indoctrinated with traditional approaches and practiced them with reverence. The process often involved silently watching the demonstrations done by the masters, frantically trying to record the observations through notes, and dutifully trying to copy the masters' works at home. Rarely would a master speak, much less offer instructions. I recall that once one of the masters did grin and comment how clever was a dot which he just made. I was so excited that I put three asterisks on my notes about that dot.

Because I received my Ph.D. in the United States, I have also learned to appreciate some of the merits of Western methodology and technology in teaching. What celebration this is: to own a culture that is so richly embodied with spirituality and then to have photographs, typewriters, computers, and video equipment to use. Alas, when it comes to brush painting, I know what I am talking about. I have to share.

Brush painting, up to now, has remained a mystery to many art lovers in the West. Even the Chinese find it difficult to approach. My friend, Liang Dan-feng (梁丹丰), is a gifted artist in both Chinese and Western art. She was frustrated in her bamboo studies and went to the leading master, who offered this advice: "Paint where you should, and leave space where you ought to." She later told me, "How can anyone get anything out of this!?"

I have had the privilege of teaching in the United States for over fifteen years. I recall in the early days, when I was on cloud nine elaborating profound spirituality, my students always managed to bring me down to earth by asking, "But, Ning, which way does the stroke go? What brush should I use? How wet?" To the amateur and professional alike, this manual will provide answers to all these questions. Still, please allow me to indulge in bringing you the spirit, the philosophy, the story, the history, and all the happy serendipities which make me a brush painter. Maybe someday, I can even be in a position to say "Paint where you should."

Acknowledgments

On the first day of filming the television series "Chinese Brush Painting, with Ning Yeh," three students came to witness the grand event. I noticed one lady disappeared after greeting me on the set. "Where is Maria?" I asked. "She felt so sick with nervousness for you, she had to go to the ladies room," the other two responded. When the filming ended, I heard loud cheers coming from the third floor of the building in the telecourse division. Such is the heart-felt caring and support given by my students and my school.

I wish to thank Ron Berggren, Director of Instructional Services, who initiated the idea of the television series. The support of President Vega and Associate Deans Ed Decker, Chet Platt, and Dan Casey of Coastline College eased the burdens of the double duties of a full-time instructor working on a major project.

Leslie Purdy had the vision to turn a small production into a full telecourse. It is quite unthinkable for an artist to be blessed with such a wonderful opportunity. It is even more incredible to find the realization of this opportunity assisted by people who are sincere, professional, and creative. Something classic is in the making, because of the people involved in the production. Assistant Dean David Stone has been a superb coproducer. Marilyn Clark, Resource Development Specialist, coordinated the fund-raising activities; and Marketing Manager Jim LeMay will see to it that this series gets the attention it deserves throughout the country.

The filming of the series in the Coastline Cable Center has been remarkably smooth. I thank God for sending such a gifted talent as David Hamilton, our director. I am even more gratified to have his Emmy Award-composing skill to score the music for our series. Ted Boehler has exerted extraordinary effort in supervising the operation of the studio. Dave Ettel managed the control room with great care. Tape operator John Royston and camera specialists Kevin Clark, Dan Williams, and Jerry Hein are superb artists in their own right. I thank George Waite for his editing skills, Cathy Hatfield and Julie Melcher for their assistance.

Mickey Jackson has been the heart and soul of this project. She has spent countless hours in helping to prepare the manuscripts for my album and this instructional guide. She has participated in every phase of the production. She is always there urging for the best and fastest solution to every problem. I am especially grateful for her care and respect toward the originality of my works. One note she wrote to the editor reads:

"I know the grammar is not perfect, but this is Ning!"

I thank Michael Werthman and Judith McDuff for their editing work on the instructional guide. I shall always remember the night Judi, Marjorie, Lois, and I spent together before I flew to the Orient — tightening the loose ends of the manuscript.

I wish to thank Ho Kung-shang (何恭上) of Art Book Company, a true friend. I am impressed with Mr. Liang (梁明宗) and Mr. Wong (王俊華) of Ke-Fan (克帆) Printing in Taiwan. The intense round-the-clock work ethics of all the young people and their strive for excellence have greatly enhanced the pride I have felt for my native land.

The advisory committee of Betty and Warren Freeman, Gwen and Paul Dent, Peggy and Jack O'Mara, Mary and George Butler, Maria and Milton Nathanson, Jan Haring and Nancy Knight has heightened the enthusiastic support among my friends. Without Betty and Warren, the Silk Era will not have the resources to operate; without the generous donation from Gwen, Paul, and others, the telecourse would not have launched with such confidence.

I appreciate the support and understanding of the members of the American Artists of Chinese Brush Painting. Even with its director on leave, the association operated with smoothness, and its chapters are growing in strength.

I cannot ask for better neighbors than the Petersen family. Larry set up our art supply warehouse and his sweet wife, Peggy, has contributed greatly to the daily operation of our business.

My wife Lingchi described my daughter Jashin's gesture of embracing during the Easter break. "I am hugging my dad; he missed the egg hunt for the first time because he has to print a book in Taiwan." During the course of this project, I am constantly reminded how much love there is all around me. I do have two wonderful children: Evan and Jashin.

"If you need Ning to remember anything, talk to Lingchi." Everyone who knows me invariably arrived at this conclusion. Not that Lingchi would remind me to do things; nobody really could. It is just that she would make sure it gets done herself. The immeasurable support she has rendered is the prime reason for me to feel at ease mentally and physically during the various phases of this project.

About the Author

Ning Yeh (葉 寧) was born in Mainland China in 1946. He was given the name Ning, meaning tranquility, to celebrate the ending of the war. The Yeh family has been famed in the field of brush painting for four generations. His father, a general in the Chinese army, is internationally renowned for his horse painting.

Ning Yeh's art training started when he was seven, after the family moved to Taiwan in 1949. He daily practice included the Four Gentlemen (plum, orchid, bamboo, and mum) and calligraphy. At the age of fifteen, the focus of his training turned to horse painting, his family tradition. Two years later, he won the highest honor for his horse painting at the Chinese Youth Art Festival. He proceeded with floral and landscape paintings, and he gradually developed his own style.

Ning Yeh was elected to represent his country as a cultural delegate and ambassador of goodwill to eighteen international youth conferences. In 1969, the Deputy Secretary of State from the United States invited the young artist to come to the States for an exhibition tour. Ning Yeh accepted scholarships offered by the California State University system and the Pearl McManus Foundation, and subsequently received his Ph.D. degree with honors in the field of Asian Studies at Claremont Graduate School.

In the past seventeen years, Ning Yeh's efforts have generated an unprecedented response in Southern California. His lectures, demonstrations, classes, and exhibitions are in constant demand. A large, sophisticated audience follows his work, and a new generation of American artists and teachers of Chinese brush painting exists because of his teaching.

In 1978, a special merit award was presented to him by the mayor of Los Angeles and the California State Museum Board for his outstanding contribution to the art community. In 1978, 1980, and 1984, he accepted the invitation of the prestigious Pacific Cultural Foundation of the Republic of China and organized exhibition tours to the Orient for his students. His native country responded by bestowing its highest honors and praise upon him and his students. In 1981, Ning and his wife, Lingchi, founded the American Artists of Chinese Brush Painting (AACBP). This nonprofit organization is open to all people interested in Chinese brush painting.

Ning Yeh has been featured in many television programs. In 1982, the NBC television network produced a half-hour special on his works. In this documentary, entitled "Arts of Asia," his segment was nominated for an Emmy award. The same year, he published his first art album, *The Art of Chinese Brush Painting.*

Along with their family and friends, Ning and Lingchi established OAS, Inc. (Oriental Art Supply). Over the past fifteen years, Ning Yeh has made numerous trips to the Orient. He has given personal supervision and worked side by side with brush makers, ink, color, and rice paper manufacturers to ensure the quality of their products. Ning Yeh's OAS has developed an impeccable reputation as supplier of the finest material for Chinese brush painting through direct mail and serving as a wholesale distributor in the United States.

Ning Yeh is a founding faculty member and full-time art instructor at Coastline Community College in Fountain Valley, California.

In 1987 Ning Yeh became the first Chinese brush painter to appear in an instructional television series in the United States. Chinese Brush Painting, with Ning Yeh was produced by Coastline Community College and consists of twenty half-hour programs. It is available nationwide through educational as well as cable networks. The television series is accompanied by:

1. This book, a comprehensive step-by-step guide, *Chinese Brush Painting: An Instructional Guide;*

2. A companion study guide, *Chinese Brush Painting: A Student's Guide;*

3. The finest Chinese brush painting equipment kits; and

4. A resource book, *An Album of Chinese Brush Painting: Eighty Paintings and Ideas.*

Ning Yeh travels extensively throughout the United States, lecturing and conducting workshops on Chinese brush painting, recruiting instructors, and developing Chinese brush painting programs in various art and educational institutions.

Contents

Lesson 1
An Introduction

The Philosophy:
Contrast and Harmony

Art in China is rarely thought of as a profession; instead it is considered a way of life. Hence, the philosophy of life is also the theory of painting. Chinese brush painting reflects a total experience of two schools of thought: Taoism and Confucianism. Taoism deals with nature and its intangible spirituality; while Confucianism emphasizes relationships among people with its down-to-earth, matter-of-fact approach.

Taoism

According to the Taoist, the force which sustains the energy and balance of nature is derived from two opposing elements: yin and yang. Through constant challenge and compensation, the yin and the yang result in a spontaneous equilibrium. Such integration reflects the essence of nature, or the Tao.

The diagram of **Tai-chi** describes the fundamental state of nature, which divides the whole into two opposing halves with an S-curve in between. The symbol suggests constant interaction, and each half sends a dot to the center of the opposing half, suggesting integration (Fig. 1-1).

Fig. 1-1 Tai-chi

Chinese brush painting employs opposing forms and forces in both design and execution. The vitality of nature is presented by the constant interaction of yin and yang, and the presentation of the overall balance and integration of these forces becomes the ultimate goal in Chinese brush art.

The Taoist believes that all things in nature come from the same source and return to the same source. They may vary on the surface, but in substance they share constancy. Since the Tao of nature is shared by all, the superficial classification of form becomes meaningless. A person can be a tree, or *is* a tree, since he shares the same source of Tao with the tree.

A Taoist artist might travel to many places in an attempt to discover the common denominator within nature and himself, but he rarely would draw the actual scenery of any given place. He would not risk the possibility of restricting himself to superficial details of realistic forms. He would much rather be free to express the spiritual essence which he discovered within himself, through the inspiration of observing the objects or phenomena in which he found a sense of "common sharing."

One of my worst experiences occurred during a spontaneous television interview. The interviewer found the statement "I turn myself into a horse and do a self-portrait" unacceptable and proceeded to use the next ten minutes to press an answer from me to her question, "What type of horse is this that you are doing?" I was so ."at one with" my horse, I could have kicked her.

In order to be at one with nature, the artist's mind must be free from external distractions. The Taoist speaks of the mind at the state of "nonbeing." It is when the mind reaches absolute stillness that the distinction between the artist and everything else disappears. The universe opens up before him, and he becomes one with it.

Nature in the mind of the artist is reduced to only those elements which are essential to the revelation of Tao. Irrelevant details are excluded. Here lies the prime justification for the use of ink to represent all colors and the importance of the use of space.

The Teaching of Confucius

Confucius speaks of the benevolent relationship among people in a man-centered universe. The ultimate goal is a harmonious society which begins with family and ends with mankind.

The principle of Chinese brush painting evolves around this Confucian idea. Every element in painting is regarded as an animated human spirit. Nothing is abstract, everything is "people" with different virtues according to their assigned roles. A good painting occurs when all the elements live happily ever after together. They allow one another to develop their fullest potential, while respecting one another's respective roles.

The elements in each painting can be categorized into three groups: the line, the shape (ink or color shading), and the dot. The line is a father figure. It is bold and decisive, providing the framework with firm and steady strength. But the line alone can be harsh; it is contrasted and complemented by the shading or the ink/color wash. The wash is a mother figure: fluid, translucent, providing the substance with soft and gentle grace. The dot represents the child, and it is frequently an expression of active joy coming from a carefree spirit. When properly behaved, the dot provides meaning to empty space, breaks monotony, and tightens the relationship between the line and the shape.

In all compositions, the brush painter considers the focus of the painting as the host. It is the dominating feature, and the rest of the elements are invited by the host to reinforce, support, and provide variation or interest to his party. They are guests. The guests can fully display their own virtues, but they are not in a position to take all the attention away from the host. In the event that the host and guest need better communication, a liaison can be added. The liaison should serve only as a link, while the host and guest are the main players.

In all compositions, a flow or tendency is established. Such flow usually consists of four movements:

1. Ch'i（起）— A leader to start the movement. It is firm, decisive, and establishes the theme and orientation of the painting.

2. Ch'eng（承）— A follower to support and reinforce the leader's intentions.

3. Chuan（轉）— A "how-about-trying-this-for-a-change?" person to introduce variation and diversity.

4. Ho（合）— A unifying person to bring all the parties into harmonious agreement.

Through these movements, an interesting travelling experience is created which invites a viewer into the painting through the port of entry, leads the viewer to various folks who reside along the route of this artistic journey, and eventually directs the viewer to visit and stay with the host.

All the subjects in nature embody the ethical and spiritual qualities of the Confucian man. To paint a pine tree is to describe the kindness of an elderly gentleman. To paint a peony is to depict the regal presence of an emperor. To learn Chinese brush painting is to study a five-thousand-year-old, glorious human civilization.

Chinese brush painting is an exercise of body and mind, an all-embracing activity that influences participants in their way of life, their values, and their attitudes. Chinese brush painting promotes the balance and harmony that is life itself.

The Categories

Traditionally, Chinese brush painting is classified by subject matter. The three prominent schools are: **Flower/Bird, Landscape,** and **Animal/ Figure.**

Chinese brush painting begins with the study of the *Four Gentlemen: plum, orchid, bamboo, and chrysanthemum.* These are the initial stepping stones which lead a painter into the School of Flower/Bird or Hwa-Niel (花鳥).

In the School of Flower/Bird, the artist focuses attention on the profuse special elements to be found in nature. Inspirational excitement is presented in the combined gestures of small animals, plants, birds, insects, and marine life. In an intimate corner of a flower garden or fish pond, the spirits of joy and surprise, humor and awe, are permanently captured by brush strokes.

The counterpart of Flower/Bird is the School of Landscape. Landscape painting is referred to as Shan-Shui (山水) in China. Shan refers to the mountain and rock. Shui is the water with its ever-changing faces in the forms of mist, cloud, streams, snow, waterfall. While the Flower/ Bird School focuses on the details in nature, the Landscape deals more with the massive grandeur of the mountains and waters. The mountain represents strength and constancy in nature. Water reflects grace and the changes of nature. The most inspirational scenery is where the mountain meets water.

Chinese landscape painting is seldom a realistic rendering of a specific scene. Instead, it represents the sphere of the artist's mentality, the result of the artistic search for inner spiritual essence. The mountains and waters project a calm, peaceful and balanced state of mind. While the theme of Flower/Bird emphasizes the excitement of life, the theme of Chinese Landscape painting is tranquillity.

Animal/Figure or Tung-Wuh/Jen-Wuh (動物／人物) painting has the longest history in the practice of Chinese painting. It stresses the energy and vitality of life and symbolizes the dynamic characteristics of human aspirations.

The School of Hsieh-I

Technically, the two approaches to Chinese brush painting are the Kung-Pi (工筆) style, and the Hsieh-I (寫意) style. The Kung-Pi, or Labored Brush (Fig. 1-2), developed earlier than the Hsieh-I. In this method, fine lines are drafted and layers of colored shadings are applied. The process aims to produce a rendition close to the subject in nature and to its refined beauty. A painting takes many hours and meticulous precision to complete. I sincerely admire the fine line artists and the exquisite presentation of their art form. I myself, however, have chosen to follow the Hsieh-I School.

The Hsieh-I (Depicting Idea) style, developed by the traditional scholar-painters during the eleventh century, is currently the mainstream of Chinese brush painting. Believing that the source of nature can be found in the sphere of one's mind, the Hsieh-I artist treats all the subjects he draws as idealistic expressions of his own personality. The artist pays less attention to the exterior detail but concentrates on the inner spirit. The search is to reveal not the form but the essence of his subject. The artist depicts the idea of his subjects by revealing his thoughts, feelings, emotions, attitudes, based on his personality and experiences.

Among the Hsieh-I artists, Shih-tao (石濤 1630-1707) and his contemporary Pa Ta Shen-jen (八大山人) were among the most influential. Their **Po Mo** (潑墨 **Throw Ink**) method was the inspirational source for this manual.

The basic concept of Po Mo is that in order for a painting to show the vitality of nature, it must be executed in a lively way. The movement of the brush is completed in a simple, dynamic, powerful, and speedy manner. It seems as if the artist is "throwing ink" and colors onto the rice paper.

The Po Mo method provides the artist with an ideal tool for capturing the spontaneity of the interaction of yin and yang. The artist begins his painting without any draft or preliminary sketch lines. Strokes and colors are integrated instantly and decisively while maintaining their continuity and fluidity. Since only spontaneity is natural, the brushwork is kept in its original form without any corrective effort. Spontaneity, freedom, and honesty are some of the important principles in this method of painting. Accidents present challenges to the artist to develop new perspectives. Sometimes the first blob can be the first accident, and the rest are a desperate effort to justify that accident. Good paintings can come as unannounced sudden enlightenment, sometimes under the most unusual combination of accidents. In reality, however, the Po Mo method demands the utmost mental and physical concentration. Furthermore, it requires constant practice. Good painting can be the result of good fortune, but only a good hand and a good mind can take the best advantage when good fortune strikes.

Fig. 1-2 The Kung-Pi Style, by Yu Chung-lin

Equipment Preparation and Care

For the convenience of beginning students, I have selected two sets of equipment to accompany this guide.

The Students' Set

Contains a complete set of basic materials for Chinese brush painting; developed as an introductory set at low cost, for student practice purposes (Fig. 1-3):

    S2   Basic-Soft brush
    H2   Basic-Hard brush
    C2   Basic-Comb brush
    BI   OAS Bottled Ink
    R2a Small roll of rice paper
    Set of "Guta" Chinese painting colors: 12 tubes

The Artists' Set

Contains the following fine materials (Fig. 1-4):

    S2a Large Soft brush
    H2a Idea hard brush
    C2b Flower/Bird combination brush
    BI   OAS Bottled Ink
    4 boxes of Chinese color chips:
       red, vermillion, indigo, burnt sienna
    1 package of Chinese yellow chunks
    1 jar of poster white
    R2a Small roll rice paper

Each set contains all the necessary materials for Chinese brush painting (as shown in Ning Yeh's television series). The materials are designed so that students can use either set to start their practice. Some students may wish to begin with the Students' Set and later advance to the Artists' Set.

With the other, readily available equipment you can find around your home, these kits should enable you to produce many "masterpieces" of Chinese brush painting.

Fig. 1-3 Students' Set

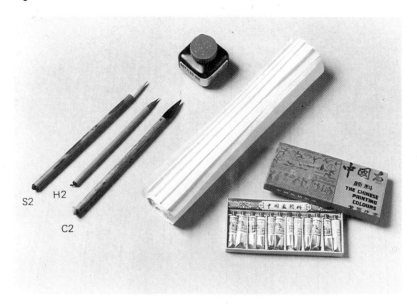

S2   H2

C2

Fig. 1-4 Artists' Set

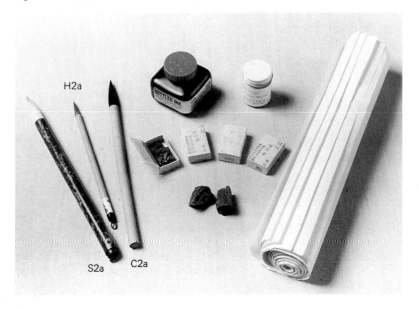

H2a

S2a   C2a

Brushes

The brushes are labeled as follows:

S: Soft brush   1: Small size
H: Hard brush   2: Average size
C: Combination brush   3: Oversized

The soft brushes are usually made of goat hair, mostly with white bristles. They are used mainly in Chinese calligraphy. I use the larger soft brushes for bamboo trunk studies.

The hard brushes are usually made of wolf hair with brown bristles. These brushes are valued for their sharp tips and bouncing resilience. I use hard brushes for all the line work and for slender shapes which come to a point.

The combination brushes are usually made of mixed hair with hard bristles inside and soft bristles outside. Combination brushes are used mostly to develop fuller shapes in floral and animal studies.

A Chart for Brush Selection

	Students' (Good)	Artists' (Better)	Masters' (Best)
Soft	Basic-Soft	Large Soft	Large Soft
Hard	Basic-Hard	Idea Big Idea*	Orchid Bamboo L. Orchid Bamboo
Comb.	Basic-Comb	Flower/Bird	Large Flow

For best results in signature, line, and dots, add the Flow.
For detail work, add the Best Detail.
For landscape line add the Landscape.
For landscape texture add the Mountain Horse.
For background shading and mist, add the Wash brush.
For extra large strokes, add the oversized Lan.

*Big Idea brush is not included in the Artists' Set. I have chosen the Idea brush because it offers finer lines.

Since the discussion in this guide is based on the equipment of the Artists' Set, and my demonstrations on television frequently include the brushes listed under the Masters', it is very important to refer to the chart above to find comparable brushes to use. Let me describe these brushes in detail:

Brushes in the Sets

The Students' Set

S2 **Basic-Soft** 1/2'' x 1-5/8'' (diameter x hair length)
The brush has a full body and even-length white goat hair; it has good absorption and is great for bamboo trunk practice.

H2 **Basic-Hard** 3/8'' x 1-1/8''
The best among the most reasonably priced wolf hair brushes.

C2 **Basic-Comb** 1/2'' x 1-3/4''
A good size brush for floral and animal studies.

The Artists' Set

S2a **Large Soft** 5/8'' x 2''
Larger, fuller, and more stable than Basic-Soft.

H2a **Idea** 5/16'' x 1-1/16''

C2a **Flower and Bird** 3/8'' x 1-1/2''
See the following discussion of "best brushes."

Best Brushes

The soft brushes included in our set are among the best in their category. There are several series of hard and combination brushes which are among the treasures in Chinese brush painting. I am using some of these brushes for my demonstrations on television. For more advanced work, I recommend the following brushes:

Hard Brushes

The Idea Series

The Idea series of hard brushes are excellent line brushes with sharp points and bouncing resilience. They are the most versatile brushes for all purposes.

H2a **Idea** 5/16'' x 1-1/16'' (Included in the Artists' Set)
One of the best hard brushes produced in China. Used for Four Gentlemen studies — orchid, bamboo, mum, plum; as well as for small flower petals and line work for all subjects, especially veins and twigs. The brush has a fine tip to handle details such as pollen dots and stamens.

H2b **Big Idea** 3/8'' x 1-3/16''
This brush handles all the tasks of the Idea brush. With a fuller body, it is able to produce larger shapes with more color variations. The Big Idea brush is used for leaves, branches, and petals.

The Orchid Bamboo Series

The name Orchid Bamboo is given to this series of brushes because of their incomparable ability to deliver the blade-type leaves which grace the orchid and bamboo.

H2c **Orchid Bamboo** 3/8'' x 1-3/8''
The ultimate hard brush for branches and blade-shaped florals.

H2d **Large Orchid Bamboo** 7/16'' x 1-7/16''
This brush functions like a larger size Big Idea.

Combination Brushes

The Flower and Bird Series

C2a **Flower and Bird** 3/8'' x 1-1/2''
The combination brush for the Artists' Set. Developed specially for producing full shapes in floral and bird studies; also great for painting animals.

The Flow Series

C2c **Flow** 3/8'' x 1-3/16''
An exquisite brush for line, dot, and calligraphy. Its flexibility allows more variety of shapes. I call it a Lady Idea brush. The tip of this brush seems to have a spirit of its own. It adds character to all the lines and dots.

C2d **Large Flow** 7/16" x 1-3/4"
One of my favorite brushes for floral and animal studies (horse, panda, petal, leaf). This brush offers wider range and better flexibility than the Flower and Bird (Fig. 1-5).

Specialty Brushes

H1a **Best Detail** 3/16" x 13/16"
It is the finest detail brush, good for delicate line work, such as stamens, pine needles, bird beaks and eyes, and tiny pollen dots.

H1b **Landscape** 1/4" x 1-1/16"
The landscape brush is best for fine lines with variation, such as trees and rocks. It is a tough brush for withstanding the torturing exercises in landscape.

H2f **Mountain Horse** 7/16" x 2"
A "punk hair"-like brush made with the toughest bristles, used for texture work in landscape.

F1 **Wash Brush** 2-1/2" wide
A flat wide brush, essential for background shading.

H3 **Lan** 9/16" x 2-1/2"
An excellent oversized brush for large leaves (Fig. 1-6).

Fig. 1-5 Best Brushes

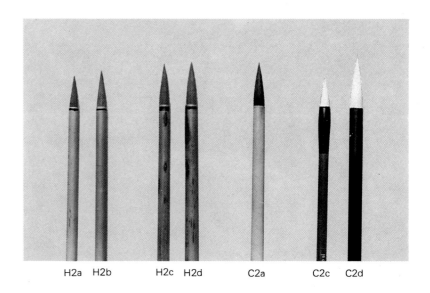

H2a H2b   H2c H2d   C2a   C2c C2d

Fig. 1-6 Specialty Brushes

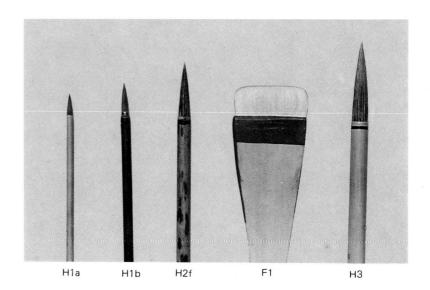

H1a   H1b   H2f   F1   H3

Brush Preparation and Care

A new brush comes with a cap to protect the bristles. This cap is useless after you have put the brush to use.

Soak the bristle portion of a new brush in cold water until the hairs become unglued. Usually, the soft and combination brushes take a longer time; the hard brush takes just a few minutes.

Rinse the brush with water after painting, wipe off the excess water with a paper towel, and regroup the tip back to a fine point. When the brush is dried, store it in a holder, wrap it with a bamboo screen, or hang it up if the handle comes with a loop.

Paper

Rice Paper

In general, rice paper can be divided into two groups: raw paper and sized paper.

Raw Paper

Most artists prefer using raw paper for floral and animal paintings, for it captures the most dynamic qualities of color blending and ink strokes in their original state.

Raw 1 **Double Shuen**

This paper has been called "the most honest" paper. It has fine absorption and is capable of reflecting the maximum range of color variations. It is best suited for the spontaneous style of brushwork. Most floral and animal paintings are done with this paper. Double Shuen comes in a large sheet (27" x 54"); a wholesale package of 100 sheets is also available.

For convenience, Double Shuen is cut into 1/4 and 1/3 of its regular size and put into a roll.

Raw 2a **Double Shuen Small Roll:** 13-1/2" x 27", 12 sheets.

Raw 2b **Double Shuen Large Roll:** 18" x 27", 12 sheets.

Raw 3 **Colored Shuen:** 18" x 27", 12 sheets.
This single-layered Shuen paper is dyed into various colors (brown, rose,

olive, and jade) and offers exciting contrast to light-colored florals or a more muted background for dark-colored florals.

Raw 4 **Practice Roll** 18" x 600"
This is machine-pressed paper which has an absorbent nature similar to Double Shuen, convenient to use for practice.

Sized Paper

Usually sizing is done to reduce the absorbent nature of the raw paper and allow the repeated application of colors and strokes. Sized paper is used most effectively for landscape and floral subjects with shaded backgrounds.

Sized 1 **Jen Ho** 24" x 40" (approximately)
The primary paper in landscape exercises.

Sized 2 **Ma** 23" x 40" (approximately)
A hemp paper, Ma shows exciting texture for line work and subjects with shaded backgrounds.

Mounting Paper

I prefer to mount the finished painting onto a type of paper which is similar to that used in watercolor paintings. I then frame the mounted painting under protective glass.

Paper Preparation and Care

Uncut large sheets should be rolled up and protected with wrapping paper. Paper should not be folded, unless one intends to cut along the folded line.

Ink

Chinese brush painting begins with black and white studies. Even in color studies, ink remains a vital feature. Ink gives substance to a painting and develops the volume of contrast.

Good ink produces the darkest black. It is smooth and blends with water without any residue. It has a velvety shine and can be fully absorbed into rice paper. When it dries, it becomes permanent; rewetting and mounting will not cause ink to run. Blended with water, good ink can present a great range of shades. Except for the darkest shades, ink is transparent and blends easily with other colors.

Ink Stick

Traditionally, ink was produced by grinding an ink stick with water onto an ink stone. The ink stick is the source of ink, and it is made of pine soot or lamp black, then mixed with glue into a stick.

Ink Stone

The ink stone is often made of slate. For painting purposes, the best-shaped slate is square with a deep circular well and a drainage spout for draining excess water or ready-made ink. The stone comes with a cover to prevent ink from evaporating. The cover is also sometimes used to grind a small amount of thick ink.

Ink Preparation and Care

To make ink, put 2 or 3 teaspoons of water into the well of the ink stone. Hold the ink stick vertically and grind it slowly with a circular motion. The ink is ready when the water becomes thick and turns the darkest color. Test the ink with a dry brush. If the ink still runs on the rice paper, more grinding is needed. Prepare fresh ink for each painting exercise. After grinding, wipe off the ink on all sides of the ink stick with a paper towel. After practice, wash the ink stone thoroughly. Old or dry ink loses its ability to mix with water.

Bottled Ink

Ready-made bottled ink is easy to use and convenient to carry; it has replaced the ink stick and stone to a large extent and is favored by both painters and calligraphers.

BI **OAS Bottled Ink:** Included in Students' and Artists' Sets.
BB **Brown Bottle:** The finest ready-made ink.
BC **Ceramic Jar:** The ultimate (Fig. 1-7).
Vermillion Ink: It is used as an alternative to black ink exercises.

Fig. 1-7 Ink Stick, Ink Stone, and Bottled Ink

Color

Chinese Chip Colors

The Chinese chips produce the best colors to use with rice paper. They include chunks of **yellow** and boxes of **burnt sienna, indigo, red, vermillion** (included in the Artists' Set). All of these colors work with water just as watercolors do. They are not good for human or animal consumption. One really should keep them away from children and pets.

Chinese Chip Color Preparation and Care

To prepare these colors, pour the entire contents of each color package into an individual dish. Separate the yellow pieces, with more in one (clean yellow) and less in the other (to mix with indigo to produce green, or "dirty yellow"). Slightly tilt the dish so the color chips can gather to one side. Put 3 or 4 drops of water onto the color chips and gently shake the dish until all the chips are touched by water. When they are dry, all of the chips will be glued onto the dish.

Before each painting session, put 2 to 4 drops of water into each dish to soften the colors according to needs. Colors will be softened in 2 minutes.

After use, allow the colors to dry before stacking these dishes. This will help prevent the growth of fungus. Should fungus appear, rinse it off so people do not know that you have not been practicing. An odor may develop, but the color is still good.

Guta Chinese Painting Colors

A student may use the following tubes from the Students' Set as substitutes for the traditional chips and chunks: **Gamboge Tint** (yellow), **Ochre** (burnt sienna), **Cyanine** (indigo), **Bright Red** (red), **Vermillion Tint** (vermillion), **Sky Blue** (sky blue). In addition, **Peony Red, Rouge Tint,** and **Cinnabar Tint** are good supplements to red; the **Azurite** and **Mineral Green** are very useful in landscape paintings. The set also includes a tube of **White.** The tubes are factory-sealed; use a thin nail to push a hole at the top of the tube to let the color out. The tube material is really primitive, but the colors are okay, and the cost is really reasonable.

Poster White

The **OAS Artists' Poster White** is bottled specially for Chinese brush painting. A student may also use **Dr. Martin's Flo 2** and/or **Pelikan's concentrated designers color 730/50.** The white is kept in the original jar.

Western Watercolors

Besides the Chinese colors, a number of **Winsor & Newton watercolors** have been successfully adopted. Among them are **crimson lake, purple madder, permanent magenta, brown madder,** which can be used to supplement red; and **French ultramarine, Winsor violet, neutral tint** used for blue-purple. In landscape, **yellow ochre** is used for land, **cerulean blue** for sky and water, **Winsor emerald & Prussian green** for green, **managanese blue** for bright blue, and **charcoal gray** for shading.

It is best to use all the watercolors fresh from the tube.

Other Equipment and Materials Needed

Color Dishes

Each of the Chinese colors needs an individual container so it can stay clean for repeated use. The porcelain **"Color Dishes"** in a set of 5 are the best containers. It is a good idea to order extra dishes so the yellow chunks can be separated into 2 containers: One is used to mix with indigo to produce green; the other stays clean.

Saucers

Four or more white saucers for mixing. The porcelain **Flower-shaped Plate** is best suited for handling watercolors. Its weight keeps it from shifting, and it is deep, which prevents different colors from mixing together.

Water Containers

One container for rinsing ink and another for other colors are needed. Do not use a tall container, as one should be able to see the water in the container and examine how deeply the brush is dipping. The porcelain water container with 3 divisions is ideal (Fig. 1-8).

Fig. 1-8
The Most Useful Porcelain Wares: Color Dishes, Flower-shaped Plate, and Three-divisioned Water Container.

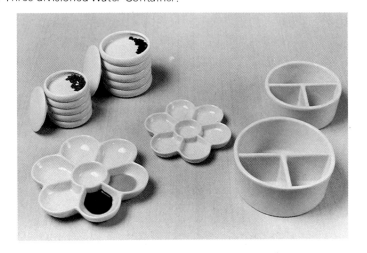

Felt

A piece of felt, cut to cover the entire painting area of the table, is the ideal material to place under the rice paper to prevent the excess moisture from forming a stain on the painting. Felt material is available at most fabric stores.

Paper Towels

A roll of paper towels is needed for wiping off the excess water or color on the brush, for testing the color and moisture, and for grouping the brush tip.

Other Accessories

A spray bottle (fine mist)
Paper weights
A pair of scissors or a **paper cutter**
Masking tape
A notebook and **pen** or **pencil** to record new findings
A brush stand to rest brushes on
A book stand to rest study materials on

Studio Setup

Chinese brush painting is done by having the paper lay flat on the table. Holding the brush vertically, the artist may sit or stand to paint. You should have a surface at least as big as a card table or a larger rectangular table. Spread your felt in the painting area. Place the equipment alongside your painting hand. Set the water container at the top, so that it is reachable by your hand and you can see the brush tip working with water. Place your ink stone or ink dish and your set of Chinese colors below the water container. Next place the saucers for mixing and/or a plate for watercolors. Fold 2 or 3 paper towels and tuck them underneath the saucer. Place your brushes on top of the towels.

It is conceivable that you may sometimes be watching television while you paint. I suggest you position your television set to the side of your painting equipment. Have the art album on a book stand above the painting area and this guide and a small notebook right next to you (Fig. 1-9).

Fig. 1-9 Studio Setup

For more information on Chinese brush painting instructional books and art albums, materials and supplies, signature and seals, please request the "OAS Catalog" from Ning Yeh's Art Studio, 10181 Crailet Drive, Huntington Beach, California 92646. Telephone: (714) 962-5189 or (714) 963-5429.

Lesson 2
Orchid, Part 1:
Leaves

How to Hold and Load the Brush

Before we begin our orchid lesson, let us invite our new brush to become part of our body and spirit.

How to Hold the Brush

Fingers

Use the first section of your thumb and index finger to hold the middle section of the brush handle. Pick up the brush and maintain the handle in a vertical position.

Slide the middle finger downward a little from the index finger so that its first section presses against the front of the handle.

Bring the ring finger to the back of the brush handle, with the base of the nail pushing against the handle.

Place the small finger next to the ring finger, however, the small finger need not make contact with the handle of the brush (Fig. 2-1).

Fig. 2-1 Correct Finger Positions

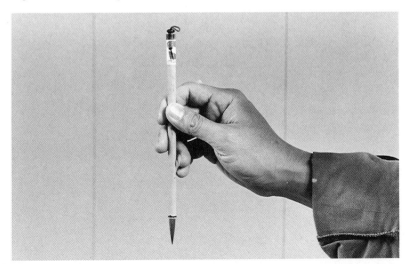

After placing all five fingers, try to use the middle finger and the ring finger to pull and push the handle back and forth a little. Then, use the thumb with the index and middle finger to roll the handle side to side a little. Gradually, all five fingers will become adjusted to these movements.

As you begin to feel comfortable, this will become the natural positioning of all your fingers. If you still feel awkward, too bad! You have to get used to it; it is the only way. Some of you may think that you can get away with holding the brush as if you are holding a pencil. DON'T! Your work would tell the whole world that you were not holding the brush the right way.

In most cases, you should hold the handle at its middle section. For more detailed works, move the fingers lower. For freer motion, move the fingers higher.

How much strength should one exert on the fingers to hold the brush? Most masters believe that one should hold the brush as if it were a weapon, with strength. The old tutor had the habit of sneaking up behind his students to try to pull brushes out of their hands. Those who failed to grab their brush tightly would have ink stains on their fingers. At the end of the session, those who had the most ink stains would receive corporal punishment. Those were the good old days of teacher supremacy. On the other hand, when Master Wang Tsi-tzu (王羲之 A.D. 321-379, Tang dynasty, considered by many as the foremost calligrapher in Chinese history) demonstrated his art of calligraphy, the record showed that during the excitement of a large bold stroke, "the brush came flying out of his hand." Obviously he did not hold the brush tightly.

I would advise my students to hold the brush firmly at first and develop the habit. After a while, the brush becomes so much a part of one's body that one is no longer aware how much strength is exerted.

Palm

While the finger exerts a firm grasp on the brush handle, your palm should be left open and airy, not closed tightly. The old tutor used to ask pupils to hold fresh eggs in their palm while holding their brushes. It is the "roominess" of the palm which allows the freer movement of the fingers.

Wrist

For freer movement, straighten your wrist in relation to your hand. For firmer and more detailed strokes, bend your wrist to add more stability.

Arm

For larger, freer movements, your arm must be lifted off the table. The old tutor used to require a beginning pupil to balance a glass of water on top of the elbow to make sure the elbow was not lowered during painting. For detailed work and controlled studies which require precision, you may rest your wrist on the paper and use your fingers to draw (you can see I am, after all, a very reasonable person).

Have I ever tried any of the old tutor's methods on my students? In the Southern California college environment, this would leave me with no students.

The Right Posture: The Five Straights

Chinese brush painting requires the right posture, which can be described by the principle of "Five Straights."

Sit Straight

Sit with shoulders leveled, one hand holding the brush vertically aligned with your head, the other arm resting on the table to secure the paper. Legs should be spread naturally, with both feet on the ground. Do not cross your legs.

For larger paintings, a standing position is preferred. Stand with one foot in front of the other, one hand securing the paper, the other hand holding the brush.

Head Straight

Your face should be facing forward gently, looking down on the paper without turning your neck.

Body Straight

Keep your chest out, your back straight.

Brush Straight

Unless you have been told otherwise, always maintain your brush handle in a vertical position. During each stroke, move your arm, not your fingers, to maintain the vertical position of the brush.

Heart Straight

Concentrate and remain sincere, honest, and calm. Be confident and positive.

Among the five straights, four can be witnessed physically. I also have developed full confidence that all my students over the years also have their hearts straight. I suspect the "crooks" might be taking courses in Business Administration or Politics instead of Chinese Brush Painting.

How to Load the Brush

Forming a Tip

Oriental brushes are unique in that when the bristles are wet they group into a remarkable point. This point, when formed correctly and properly guided, becomes the artist's soul and spirit. All of the brushes in our selection are the finest, and they perform miracles if they are handled right.

Before each painting exercise, soak the entire bristle portion of the brush in the water. Stroke the brush a few times along the edge of the water container to get rid of some of the excess moisture. At this point you will have the ideal amount of moisture on the brush for subjects which require a "wet" brush.

In most cases, however, you should tap and stroke the bristles on the paper towel to wipe off the excess water. Turn the handle by lifting it away from the paper towel from time to time to allow all sides of the bristles to dry. In this process, try to group the hairs into a fine point. Always wipe with the bristles trailing the handle. Never wipe sideways.

Some students do not realize the vital importance of keeping all the hairs straight while forming a tip. They roll the brush while the tip is in contact with the edge of the water container or on top of the paper towel, and the hairs become curled and spiralled. Such a "fake" tip would develop split ends during stroke practice.

This initial preparation of the brush serves several purposes: it forms a fine tip; it gets rid of trapped moisture; and it solidifies the bristle body to help the tip stay pointed and bouncing.

In later discussion, whenever references are made to loading the brush, the above-mentioned process has been assumed.

Loading the Moisture

After the tip is formed, redip the tip into water. The length to be submerged into water varies according to the painting subjects but rarely exceeds half of the bristle length. The most common problem of beginning students in brush painting is finding the stroke "too wet." It is important to always observe how deeply you are putting the tip of the brush into the water. After dipping, again stroke a few times along the edge of the water container before you load the ink or colors onto the brush.

Load the ink or colors with the same care by stroking along the edge of an ink well or color dish to prevent excessive moisture and to allow the natural grouping of the tip to stay undisturbed.

You are now mentally and physically ready to paint.

Fig. 2-2

Lan

(One Flower, One Stem)

Hui

(One Stem with Multiple Flowers)

The Idea of Orchid

To study the grass orchid is to appreciate the beauty of lines and their interrelationship with the beauty of space. The tip movement of the brush reflects the integrated whole of the artist's mind, hand, arm, and body. Orchid painting represents the ultimate expression of the "running style" of Chinese calligraphy (Fig. 2-3). It is a joyful, spontaneous movement that signifies the essence of a carefree spirit.

Fig. 2-3 Lan Shown in Four Styles of Chinese Calligraphy:

Seal Style,   Li Style,   Running Style, and Regular Style

The orchid is a happy spirit. Its Chinese character is comprised of a grass top (艹), a symbol of gateway (門), and a note of invitation (柬). The character suggests the plant extending its welcoming arms, cheerfully inviting people to enter the gate of spring. The artist's mood should be in a state of joyful ecstasy. It was said that Master Chen Pan Ch'iao (鄭板橋 1693-1763) painted most of his orchids when he was half drunk. It needs to be noted here, however, that one must paint the orchid with a clear mind. For Chen, a well-known drunk, being *half* drunk might have been in some of his most wakeful moments.

The grass orchid is a symbol of the yin virtue — the ultimate spirit of female grace. With its form full of soft curving lines, it swings joyfully in the spring breeze. Yet such graceful softness does not imply weakness, hesitation, or fear. It is this exquisite balance between the delightful, carefree, feathery touch and the measured, firm, and decisive movement that produces the finest outcome. To produce a good orchid painting requires constant practice; beyond that, certain measures of good fortune need to surface. One can never *expect* to do a good orchid painting. It just occurs every now and then. When it does, let us bring out the fine wine and celebrate the occasion.

Orchid painting reveals many of the fundamental concepts of composition. Through painting the orchid, the artist acquires knowledge of the distribution of shapes and spaces; the establishment of the tendency or the flow of the painting; the host and guest relationship; and the balance and teamwork among the various elements of the painting. The orchid has one of the simplest of all the forms. Yet, because of its simplicity, it is one of the most difficult subjects to master, since every flaw is painfully obvious.

The grass orchid is mostly admired for its subtle beauty. Its fragrance is intimately enticing but never overpowering. It usually chooses its hermitage in the most spiritual places in nature, where mountain is embraced by the mists or rocks by the roaring stream. To sit with an orchid is a scholarly pursuit with long tradition, one that inspires purity and simplicity.

Ch'u Yuan (屈原), the most commemorated poet of the ancient Chu (楚 about 300 B.C.) always wore an orchid on his robe to set himself apart from the corrupted ministers. In the year 278 B.C., on the fifth day of the fifth moon, he drowned himself in protest against the ill-advised emperor. The local people raced down the river by boat, in vain trying to salvage his body. They beat gongs and drums to scare off the "evil spirits" in the water and threw rice wrapped with bamboo leaves to calm the creatures in the waters. This day has since been commemorated in the celebration of the Dragon-Boat Festival. Many orchid societies hold shows in memory of Ch'u Yuan.

The Anatomy of the Orchid

Petals. There are five petals, with two short ones forming the center and three longer ones around the perimeter. The center petals stand vertically from the stem, embracing each other. The perimeter petals, resembling a set of propellers, surround the center.

Stamens. The center column, the stamens, consists of both male and female structures. (I really do not care what its name should be, no chauvinism is implied here.) The Chinese artist prefers to interpret the stamens as a group of "happy dots" instead of as a solid shape. Connected in spirit, one dot leads to another and eventually ends in the center base of the flower.

Stem. This is perpendicular to the base of the flower and reaches into the center of the leaf cluster.

Sheath. A protective skin wrapping each of the growth sections along the stem, the sheath is the orchid artist's all-purpose remedy to "rescue" the monotonous shape of the stem.

Leaves. Each cluster of leaves is rooted into one base. The roots of the leaves resemble a group of Fishes Looking for the Same Food.

Fig. 2-4 Elements of the Orchid

Materials and Preparation

Paper: Double Shuen or the Practice Roll.

Brushes: Use the Idea (H2a) brush from the Artists' Set, or the Basic-Hard (H2) brush from the Students' Set.

Ink: Use OAS Bottled Ink. Put about 5 teaspoonfuls into one saucer and put one drop into a separate dish, allowing it to dry a little to be used as the pasty ink.

Brush, Moisture, and Ink Value Chart

The fractions below refer to the length of the brush bristle from the tip upward. For instance, under moisture, "1/3" means you should dip about 1/3 of the length of the brush hair into water.

Element	Brush	Moisture	Ink Value
Leaves	Basic Hard or Idea	wet 1/3	dark
Petals	Basic Hard or Idea	wet tip only 1/6	light body (clear water) pasty at the very tip
Stem and Sheath	Basic Hard or Idea	what is left on your brush after painting the petals	medium-light
Stamens	Basic Hard or Idea	wet tip with ink only (no water)	pasty at the tip

For further studies on the orchid, the best equipment is:
for leaves, use Big Idea (H2b), or Orchid Bamboo (H2c);
for petals, use Idea (H2a), or Best Detail (H1a);
for stamens, stem, and sheath, use Flow (C2c) or Idea.
Freshly ground ink produces a better quality pasty ink than the bottled ink.

Step-by-step Instruction

Leaves

Key Ideas

Begin each leaf from the root, moving upward and outward. The brush tip travels in the middle of each leaf stroke. Make sure the brush tip trails the brush handle and points opposite the direction of the stroke. Use your arm to move the brush, maintain the vertical position of the brush, and deliver the stroke without waving the brush handle.

Each leaf is one curve, with no waves. Each leaf starts with medium or no pressure; then increase and relax the pressure one or two times during the stroke (no more than twice). Maintain at least a medium pressure during the middle of the stroke, except when the leaf is turning, so the width can carry the weight of the leaf. Allow enough distance so that you can taper the pressure to a fine point toward the end. Do not end abruptly. "Follow through," like an airplane taking off at the end of the stroke.

The brush movement begins a little earlier than the root point, "gliding" down like an airplane landing. Move the brush with a steady speed, not too fast or too slow. Leaves in the middle of the cluster can begin with a firm "planting" of the brush tip to show their roots. Leaves on the sides begin without pressure.

It is a good idea to bend the tip slightly in the direction opposite the direction of the stroke to allow a smoother "landing." Be sure to adjust the tip position whenever changing directions so that the tip always points opposite to the direction of the stroke.

Basic Strokes

Loading the Brush

Form the tip (check the section "How to Load the Brush" above), dip the tip 1/3 length into the water, stroke the excess off along the water container, then load more than 1/2 the bristle length with dark ink. Bristles should be wet to the point that the body expands a little.

First Stroke

This stroke is the host, the leader that develops the orientation or flow. It begins with light pressure, increases to medium pressure, tapers, increases more, then gradually tapers to a fine point (Fig. 2-5).

Second Stroke

The second stroke reinforces the host and develops the "Phoenix Eye." It begins with less pressure and starts pressure earlier than the first stroke, then tapers to allow the brush tip to regroup to a fine point. Change direction to cross the first stroke, make sure the tip stays in the middle, increase pressure, then taper to a natural end (Fig. 2-5).

The Phoenix Eye is the space formed by the two strokes and is the focal area of crucial importance. The pleasing shape resembles the smiling eye of a Chinese opera singer, or the mystical bird which frequently acts as the happy playmate of the Chinese dragon (Fig. 2-5).

Fig. 2-5 First and Second Strokes with Phoenix Eye

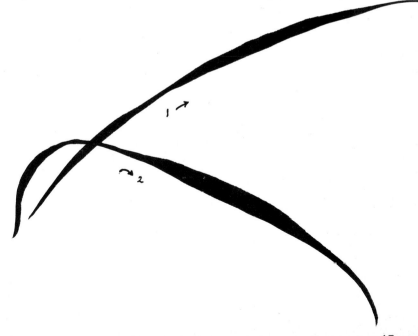

Note that the starting portion of the first stroke should not curve too much, as the orientation needs to be firmly established for the rest of the leaves to follow. See Fig. 2-6A for a "Bum Leader."

Notice that the second stroke starts lower and loops lower than the first stroke. Do not make the two strokes the same height (Fig. 2-6B).

Too large or too small a Phoenix Eye can definitely ruin your orchid (Figs. 2-6C, 2-6D).

The roots of the two strokes should be formed as though they were Fishes Looking for the Same Food. This principle should be observed throughout the composition. It suggests the unity of the leaf cluster, that all the leaves tuck into one bulb. You should never see one fish collide into another (Fig. 2-6E), or fish get lost on the way home (Fig. 2-6F).

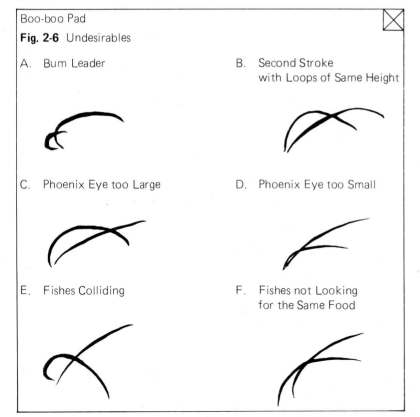

Boo-boo Pad

Fig. 2-6 Undesirables

A. Bum Leader

B. Second Stroke
   with Loops of Same Height

C. Phoenix Eye too Large

D. Phoenix Eye too Small

E. Fishes Colliding

F. Fishes not Looking
   for the Same Food

Third Stroke

This stroke provides change and develops the height of the leaf structure. It starts between the two previous strokes (both in width, and in height), and is at first allied closely with the first stroke, to show respect of its leadership. Then the stroke pulls away and upward (Fig. 2-7).

Fig. 2-7 Third Stroke

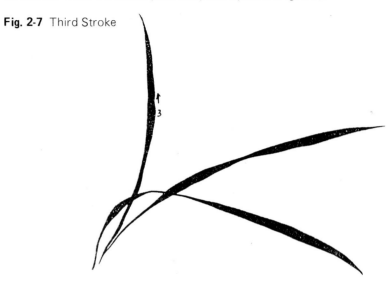

The third stroke should pull away only after following the leader for a while, otherwise, the whole composition is split into two (Fig. 2-8A). Also, try not to alter the starting point of the root too much. The unreasonable height of the root makes it appear to hang in the air (Fig. 2-8B).

Boo-boo Pad

Fig. 2-8

A. Third Stroke Pulling Away
   from First Stroke too Soon

B. Third Stroke Rooted too High

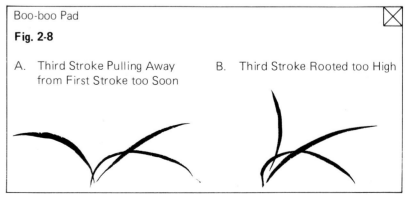

Fourth and Fifth Strokes

These strokes balance, adjust, tuck, and unify the whole composition. They should be shorter, skinnier, more straightforward than the previous strokes to show their youthful outlook. Avoid forming the fourth and fifth strokes with identical attitudes, shapes, and angles (Fig. 2-9).

Fig. 2-9 The Completion of the Five Leaves Exercise

Place the starting points of the fourth and the fifth strokes to form the most pleasing arrowhead shape to the whole root cluster. If the cluster is too flat near the root, plant the roots of these strokes higher (Fig. 2-10A). If the cluster is too sharp near the root, plant the roots of these strokes lower (Fig. 2-10B).

Fig. 2-10 Roots of the Side Strokes

A. Side strokes rooted high   B. Side strokes rooted low

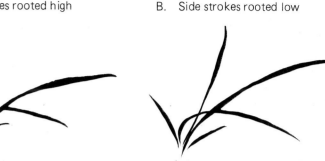

Additional Leaves

To avoid congestion, try to establish a new cluster for additional leaves, rather than keep adding onto the same group. Use the small leaf to cross into the first group as a liaison or bridge to link the cluster. Use the larger leaf on the outside to guide the new cluster back into the first. Additional clusters can be rooted higher to develop the proper depth. The center cluster usually is closer; hence, it is rooted lower (Fig. 2-11).

Fig. 2-11 Orchid Leaf Cluster with Additional Leaves

Avoid the following problems in composition (Fig. 2-12):

Boo-boo Pad

Fig. 2-12 Common Problems in Leaf Composition

A. Parallel lines

B. Identical wings

C. Tic-Tac-Toe, ( ) two lines crossing two lines

D. Fence, ( ) one line crossing three or more lines

E. Having three or more tip points forming a line

F. Chicken Foot, three or more lines crossing or joining at one point

G. Loose Bottom, too scattered near the root

H. Bonded Foot, too tight near the root

Now that you have mastered the leaves of the orchid, it is time to consider the flower. We will do this in Lesson Three.

Lesson 3
Orchid, Part 2:
Flowers

Fig. 3-1

Warning against Premature Celebration

If you are elated with your initial success in Lesson One, consider it "beginner's luck." Instead of the roaring laughter you now feel inside your heart, I'd like you just to wear a Mona Lisa type of grin. Get hold of yourself and your brush.

In the orchid exercise, each element has a different attitude. The leaf exercise in Lesson 1 reflects a spontaneous, free-flowing spirit of letting go. In this flower lesson, however, the petals show a delicate, more refined gentleness. Although each petal displays a delightful, dancing quality, the strokes are done with considerable measure of control. Be very careful in getting the right amount of moisture, ink, and pressure.

Step-by-step Instruction

The Flower Petals

Key Ideas

Begin each petal from the outside inward, that is, from the tip to the root. Bend most of the petals inward so that they embrace the center. Think of the symbols for parentheses () when doing these strokes (Fig. 3-2).

Fig. 3-2 Parentheses Embracing

21

Practice Strokes

Ink

The ink should be thick. If you use bottled ink, try to tilt the ink saucer slightly to create a "shoreline" area of ink, allowing it to dry a little before using. Or put one drop into a separate area and allow it to dry a little to be used as the pasty ink. The idea is to keep the ink shallow so you do not load too much of it on your brush tip.

If you use the ink stick and stone, grind the stick using two drops of water into pasty ink on the slate cover.

Loading the Brush

Use the Idea (or Basic-Hard) brush. First form the tip, then dip one-sixth of the tip's length into water, stroke the excess off along the side of the water container, and dip the very tip (about 1/16") into the pasty ink. It is important to wet only the brush tip; the bristle body should remain dry.

Do a few test strokes. If you have loaded correctly, the ink will be used up after each stroke and you will need to reload the tip before the next stroke.

The "New Moon" Shape

Begin with no pressure to show a fine point, then immediately exert slight pressure as you move into the stroke. Allow the pressure to taper into a fine point at the end of the stroke. Notice the "fat" portion is in the upper middle; the tail end is slender and graceful (Fig. 3-3A).

The Reversed-S-Curve

Begin with no pressure to produce a fine point, then immediately exert slight pressure as you move into the stroke. Meanwhile, curve the movement; reduce the pressure with a reverse curve and taper the petal to a fine point (Fig. 3-3B).

I want to explain a little more about the reversed S-curve. This is a very important stroke, and we use it as a foundation for many floral studies.

The reversed S-curve is an easier stroke for right-handed artists than for left-handed artists. I'd like you to pay attention to the direction changes of this stroke. For example, if we begin by pointing the bristle tip to 10 o'clock upon landing, then we turn the movement to the 6 o'clock

direction while exerting pressure. Finally, we lift the pressure and turn the movement to about 5 o'clock.

Another way to study the movement is to pay attention to the route which the tip travels. I like to use a speedboat on Lake Tahoe to illustrate the tip movement to my California students. In the reversed S-curve, the boat (brush tip) travels more along the western shore (California side) of Lake Tahoe.

The S-Curve

This is an easier stroke for the left-handed artist. You need to reverse all the considerations. For instance, the boat travels more along the eastern shore (Nevada side) now (Fig. 3-3C).

Fig. 3-3 Practice Strokes

A. New Moon   B. Reversed S-Curve   C. S-curve

To be precise, this is not a typical S (or reversed S). The upper portion is much shorter than the lower portion. In this way, the petal embraces the center like parentheses (). If the upper portion is long, the petal will appear to be tortured and bend in an unnatural position (Fig. 3-4).

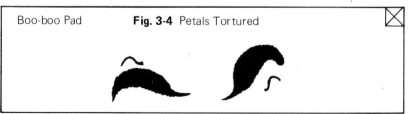

Boo-boo Pad   **Fig. 3-4** Petals Tortured

These strokes look painfully easy; yet, I could not do them for the longest time. I had nightmares and almost thought of quitting. I remember crying over these little strokes, which presumably suggest joy and happiness. I was only seven years old then. How could I possibly know that in these tiny strokes all the essence of brush painting is represented. Technically, the orchid petal requires the right amount of moisture, ink, pressure, and speed, as well as the diversity and harmony of direction, tone, and pressure-lift. Philosophically, the stroke illustrates beginning from nonbeing and returning to nonbeing, the intricate balance between the flamboyant leaf and the delicate flower. One could write a Ph.D. dissertation on these strokes. I now know why the old masters in Chinese brush painting decided to start everyone with orchid painting. Basically, it is a torture test of endurance.

The Orchid Flower

Center

The center — or bud — is formed with two short petals embracing each other. Your stroke should be almost straight, with the tip of the petals almost in contact and the root of the petals joined into one fine point to form the base of the flower. Of the two petals, one is usually longer and one shorter. The longer one is the host petal, and it decides which way the flower will be facing (Fig. 3-5).

Fig. 3-5 Center/Bud

  Flower Facing This Way

Avoid having the two petals separated too much, resulting in a pair of "rabbit ears" (Fig. 3-6A). Also avoid bending the roots too much (Fig. 3-6B) or having the two petals leading to different points as in "fishes colliding" (Fig. 3-6C).

Boo-boo Pad	**Fig. 3-6**	
A. Rabbit Ears	B. Too Much Bending	C. Fishes Colliding

Perimeter Petals

The three perimeter petals are longer than the center petals. They reach out like propellers, embracing the center.

To begin forming the perimeter petals, first add a petal to each side of the center. Make these petals taller than the center petals, and show variation in length, width, shape, and angle of each petal. Guide the roots of the petals into the center, but end the roots higher than the base of the center petals. In other words, attach the perimeter petal onto the lower shoulder, not the root, of the center petals. With this formation, the base remains undisturbed and graceful. Thus the flower looks youthful and has more depth (Fig. 3-7).

Fig. 3-7 Two Side Petals

Avoid ending the petals too low (Fig. 3-8A), or having them "horn-like" — missing the base of the center petals entirely (Fig. 3-8B).

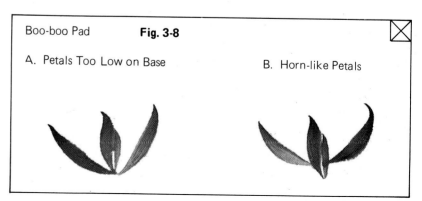

Boo-boo Pad	**Fig. 3-8**	
A. Petals Too Low on Base		B. Horn-like Petals

Finally, add a third petal to balance and complete the flower, leading its roots to join the base of the center (Fig. 3-9).

Fig. 3-9 Variations in Petal Groups

It is useful to think of the flower as an anchor, with the center two petals as its axis. When adding the perimeter petals, remember that the distribution will be one on one side, and two on the other side. The lone petal should be positioned at a wider angle to the axis, comparable to the combined angle of the two petals on the other side. The flower will then have better balance (Fig. 3-10).

Fig. 3-10 Balanced Petal Groupings

Stem and Sheath

After painting the flower petals, use the same brush and the remaining moisture and ink on the brush to draw the flower stem and sheath.

Begin the stem under the base of the center petals. Use the stem to settle the anchor of the flower in a balanced way. The stem should be completed in several sections. Pause slightly between the sections and adjust the tip position. The top section can be comparatively short and thin, the lower sections lengthened and widened. Make these sections uneven in length; the lower section need not necessarily be the longest.

The direction of the flower is determined by the longer petal in the center, so follow the tendency of the longer center petal to start the stem (Fig. 3-11A). The stem needs to carry out the wish of the flower, or the flower will have a very "sore neck" (Fig. 3-11B).

Fig. 3-11

A. Stem Direction Follows the Longer Center Petal

Boo-boo Pad
B. Flower with a Sore Neck

Lead the stem from the base of the flower into the center of the leaf cluster. End the last section of the stem by tapering above the roots of the leaf (Fig. 3-12A).

The root sheath can be either one or two strokes. The sheath can be drawn upward from the root or downward from the side of the stem. It is important to align the direction of the stem and the sheath and aim the stem at the center area of the leaf cluster (Fig. 3-12B).

Fig. 3-12 Stem, Sheath at the Center of the Leaf Cluster

A. Ending of the Stem

B. Joining of the Sheath

Notice that the sheath resembles a light, small leaf with the stem tucked into the root of the leaf. Occasionally, the sheath can shoot off along the stem to break the monotony of the stem. It is truly an all-purpose helper (Fig. 3-13).

Fig. 3-13 Sheath along the Stem

Stamen Dots

The stamen dots are the final step of the orchid painting. Like the Eye of the Dragon (Story 53, *An Album of Chinese Brush Painting: Eighty Paintings and Ideas, by* Ning Yeh), the stamen brings the spirit of the orchid to life. The stamen consists of one to three dots of varying sizes and shapes. Dip 1/16 length of the brush tip with a little moisture, then dip it into the pasty ink. When painting each dot, land the tip with a scoop pressure, similar to the motion of a quotation mark. Then lift the tip and "dance" to a second or third dot, eventually leading into the base of the flower (Fig. 3-14).

Fig. 3-14 Stamen Dots

Paint the stamen while the petals are still wet, as a little bleeding of the pasty ink into the light petal prompts more integration and spontaneity (Fig. 3-15A).

Stamen dots should usually be on the side of the shorter center petal. Think of the stamen as the flower's tongue: Do not try to make a face by sticking your tongue out from the back of the neck (Fig. 3-15B).

Be aware of the overall balance of the weight on both sides in relation to the axis of the flower. Do not overburden one side (Fig. 3-15C).

Also be aware of the value of space, especially around the base of the flower. Let the stamen leap out into the more open spaces. Do not "stuff" the petal roots (Fig. 3-15D).

Fig. 3-15 Placement of Stamen Dots

A. Perfect Harmony

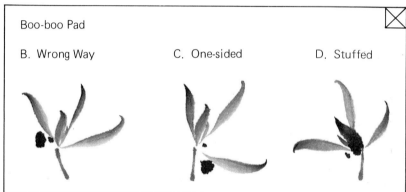

Boo-boo Pad

B. Wrong Way   C. One-sided   D. Stuffed

Two Types of Grass Orchids

Lan Orchid

The Lan orchid has only one flower on each stem and the stem is shorter than that of other orchids. The flower blossoms early in the spring. Here are examples of the Lan orchid in various stages (Fig. 3-16).

Fig. 3-16 Examples of the Lan Orchid

A. Bud

B. Partially Opened

C. Fully Opened

27

Hui Orchid

The Hui orchid has multiple flowers on each stem and the stem is longer. The flower blossoms late in the spring and continues into the summer.

To paint the Hui orchid, first draw the tip bud. Follow the root of the longer petal with your fingernail to develop a "tracing line" of the main stalk. Draw a series of flowers along and occasionally overlapping the trace. Then draw the main stalk following the trace and "leap over" the flower petals in the way. Connect the base of each flower with a stem onto the main stalk.

Teamwork Concept

You might think of the teamwork concept when composing your flower series, grouping the flowers into forward, center, and guard units:

The **forward** spearheads the whole movement. It is lightweight, penetrative, and slenderly built; it has no competitive elements to weaken its sharpness. Like a scout sent by the main unit, it should move some distance ahead.

The **center** is the largest cluster of flowers and serves as the focal point of the series. This cluster can be grouped into a host and guest composition, with occasional scouting units on its wings.

The **guard** stays not far behind the center; it reinforces the center and tapers the series to end into the root.

Be sure to balance the flowers in relation to the main stalk, left balanced with right, front balanced with back. Also, space the flowers so that the stems do not meet at one spot (the chicken foot) but alternate with intervals along the main stalk.

Design each flower to face the angle that the stem will naturally lead into the main stalk. Be careful to consider the direction of the longer center petal for each flower, so the root can swing into, instead of swing away from, the main stalk.

To enhance the depth of the cluster, save one or two flowers and add them after the main stalk is completely drawn. An example of the Hui orchid (Fig. 3-17) can be found on page 29.

Composition of the Orchid Painting

Where to Put the Flowers

When the Leaf Cluster Is Well Balanced

When the spaces around the leaves are well distributed, keep the flowers low or place the flower stems close to the leaves so that the existing space distribution suffers the least disruption.

When the Leaf Cluster Needs Help

When the leaf cluster has problems, the flowers are employed to balance the weight distribution, to develop a focus and lead the viewer's attention to the center, to enhance the flow of the leading tendency, to add new and more exciting perimeter points, to tighten or unite loose clusters, to provide contrast, and to add depth to the composition.

Orchid composition is limited only by the imagination. The following illustrations offer several examples (Figs. 3-17, 3-18).

Fig. 3-17 Hui Orchid Flower

Fig. 3-18 Orchid Composition

竹

Jwu (Bamboo)

Fig. 4-1

Lesson 4
Bamboo, Part 1:
Trunk and Branches

The Idea of Bamboo

The bamboo is the most practiced and the most important subject in Chinese brush painting. It is an expression of the yang qualities of the line: bold, decisive, and full of strength. Bamboo painting is an exercise in the "bone stroke," which provides the framework for all paintings.

Bamboo painting reflects energy. The old masters spoke of painting bamboo with a certain measure of anger in order to capture the spirit of vitality. (This probably explains why the bamboo lesson follows immediately after the orchid. For our frustrated orchid artist, the bamboo lesson should provide ample relief.) Yet the outcome of a perfectly executed bamboo invariably projects a sense of tranquility. Even a windy-day bamboo suggests a spirit of calm in the middle of a storm.

The bamboo is the most popular plant in China, and every village in southern China is surrounded by bamboo groves. To be Chinese is to feel at home with bamboo. The wandering traveller writing letters back home often mentions bamboo as a symbol for the blessings of tranquility.

In the order of the Four Gentlemen, bamboo represents the spirit of Summer. But since bamboo lasts all seasons, it is also frequently associated with pine and plum as the Three Winter Friends.

The bamboo is considered a gentleman with perfect virtues, combining upright integrity with accommodating flexibility. It represents the perfect balance of grace and strength, or yin and yang. When the storm comes, the bamboo bends with the wind. When the storm ceases, it resumes its upright position. Its ability to cope with adversity and still stand firmly without losing its original ground is inspirational to a nation which has constantly suffered calamities.

Bamboo is used in every phase of Chinese living; yet it needs very little care to grow and flourish. It is a well-sectioned plant with a polished skin and sturdy texture. Like a self-cultivated scholar in hermitage, it is ready to render services when called upon.

Since bamboo produces neither flower nor fruit, it personifies the life of simplicity. Chen Pan Ch'iao compared himself to bamboo, saying, "I will not grow flowers, so. . . I avoid tempting the butterflies and bees to disturb me."

The hollow trunk of the bamboo reminds the Chinese of humility. Artist Lin Yung praised it: "Bamboo, who understands humility by emptying his heart (without stuffing it with arrogance), is my teacher."

The young branches at the top of the bamboo trunk will not grow at the same angle as the older branches below, in order to allow sunlight for their elders. When the young shoots emerge from the roots, they are under the shade of the older bamboo. Such a pattern reflects the spirit of the young respecting the old and the old protecting the young.

The Anatomy of the Bamboo

There are numerous styles of bamboo paintings. The newborn bamboo or the sunny-day bamboo has leaves reaching upward. The windy-day bamboo has leaves carried by the breeze. The snowy bamboo, the overhanging bamboo — all have different attitudes expressed in style and composition (For samples of different styles of bamboo, please see Plates 28, 51, 70, 72 of the resource book by Ning Yeh, *An Album of Chinese Brush Painting: Eighty Paintings and Ideas.*).

In southern China, constant rain and moisture have caused the large bamboo leaves to droop. This rainy-day bamboo has been of predominant interest among brush painters and is the focus of our discussion in this lesson.

The anatomy of bamboo includes the following elements: trunk, ring, branches, and leaves.

Trunk. The root sections of the bamboo trunk are short and wide; the middle sections, up to twenty or thirty, are relatively consistent in length and width; and the top sections taper to slender and shortened shapes.

Eventually the trunk comes to a fine tip. The width changes normally take place at the ring areas. Within each section, however, the width of the trunk stays fairly constant.

Ring. The ring, or joint, circles around both ends of a section and protrudes slightly outward.

Branches. The branches are rooted in clusters at a point on top of the ring. Each cluster starts at an opposite angle from the one below it.

Leaves. The leaves are usually formed in clusters of two or more at the tip area of new branches. Leaves are connected by a short stem onto the branch. The stem may not be painted, but its "idea" — the suggestion of its presence — is there (Fig. 4-2).

Fig. 4-2 The Elements of Bamboo

Materials and Preparation

Materials and preparation for painting the bamboo are basically the same as those for painting the orchid. You need only add a soft brush.

Brush, Moisture, and Ink Value Chart

Element	Brush	Moisture	Ink Value
trunk	Basic-Soft or Large Soft	wet tip 1/4	dark on both sides fading to medium and then light at the middle
ring	Idea or Basic-Hard	dry 1/8	pasty
branch	Idea or Basic-Hard	dry 1/8	medium
leaf	Big Idea or Idea Basic-Hard	wet 1/3	topside/mature leaf; dark underside/young leaf; light shade from dark (close to viewer's eye) to light (distant)

For best results, use the Large Soft brush for the trunk, the Best Detail branch for rings, and the Orchid Bamboo brush for branches and leaves.

Step-by-step Instruction

Trunk

Key Ideas

Most bamboo studies focus only on the middle portion of the trunk. Each of the sections is relatively even in length, and it is a good idea to show only a limited number of sections. Keep the trunk simple to allow it to play a supportive role to the leaves.

Complete each trunk with one loading of the brush to insure its continuity, and project a slight overall curve.

Each section is a form of the bone stroke, which is characterized by the heavy, abrupt beginning and end to the stroke and a steady, forceful movement in between. The bone stroke is the father of all strokes.

As mentioned before, the width of the trunk should change gradually from section to section, with the lower sections wider and the top narrower, and the same width should be maintained during the course of each section. Change the width by decreasing or increasing pressure slightly at the start of a new section (Fig. 4-3).

Fig. 4-3 Trunk

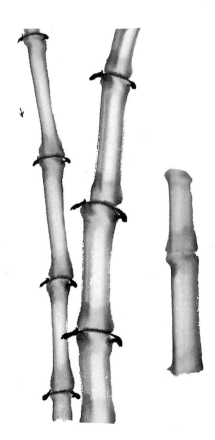

Preparation

Use the Basic-Soft or the Large Soft brush.

Prepare dark ink and slightly tilt the ink slate or saucer to create a shore-line area where ink is shallow and not in puddles. It is best to put ink in a relatively flat saucer for this exercise.

It is a good idea to start practice with your rice paper laid horizontally so that the trunk will not travel too long a distance.

Loading the Brush

Soak the entire bristle in water and use your fingers to squeeze off the moisture and flatten the tip. The flattened tip width should be a little wider than the width of the handle and should look like a "marine cut" rather than a "punk" hair style.

Dip 1/4 the length of the bristle in the water two to three times. Stroke the excess moisture off the edge of the water container. To determine whether the brush has the right amount of moistness, "test run" the entire length of the trunk on rice paper to see if the moisture can last without reloading.

Rest one side, then the other side, of the flattened tip in dark ink. To avoid overloading, gently rest the side of the bristle on the shoreline area of the ink, allowing the ink to be loaded up to 1/2 the length of the sides of the brush without running into the center area. Load both sides two to three times. Then test a stroke. You should find two dark streaks on both sides and transparent, light ink inside.

Blend the ink by pressing the tip area slightly on the saucer. You should see the dark ink on both sides start to seep into the middle.

Intensify contrast by reloading the dark ink on both sides. The desired result is a smooth transition from the dark sides to the light middle area.

Work a stroke on the paper towel to test the value and moisture on the brush. If it is too dry, dip the brush tip in the water again. If it is too wet or too dark, work a few more test strokes to reduce the moisture or ink on the brush.

For lighter trunks, just dip the brush tip 1/5 in water without reloading ink. Use the leftover ink from the darker trunk.

Movement

The stroke can be made either from top to bottom or from bottom to top. For the right-handed artist, it is easier to move down at this angle ↘ , and move up at this angle ↗ (Think of writing a check mark ✓ as you stroke).

Start each section with a little pressure; set the brush first, then begin to move. Move along each section, maintaining even pressure throughout the stroke. Use your arm to move the brush and maintain the vertical position of the brush. End each section with a little pressure, then lift the brush off the paper. Begin the next section by pushing close to the previous stroke, without leaving a gap.

Use only up to 1/4 length of the tip area to make the stroke. To assure the success of the following sections, do not allow the tip to bend too much.

Ring (Joint)

Key Ideas

If the trunk is moving to the back, the ring would be shown as a ↤ . If the trunk is moving toward the viewer, the ring would be shown as a ↢ In order to save the argument and get on with our practice, we shall show the ring as ↤ (Fig. 4-4).

The ring should be inserted while the trunk is still wet to assure integration. The brush tip is travelling in the middle of the stroke throughout all phases of the ring. Use arm, not finger movement, and hold the brush vertically. Execute the stroke with strength (Fig. 4-4).

Fig. 4-4 Ring

Preparation

Use the Basic-Hard or the Idea brush. Dip the brush tip in thick ink but keep the body dry.

Movement

The ring should be painted in one continuous movement which consists of three phases.

First Phase: Begin from the lower left corner of the top section. Let the brush tip bend slightly and point to the right. Land the tip by exerting a little pressure to the left (Fig. 4-5A).

Second Phase: Relax the pressure and allow the tip to reverse its direction. After the tip is turned, move forcefully across to the other side of the trunk with a slight bouncing leap. Reapply a little pressure after the tip has made the cross (Fig. 4-5B).

Third Phase: Relax the pressure and again allow the tip to reverse its direction. Lift the brush by tucking the end to the top right corner of the lower section (Fig. 4-5C).

Fig. 4-5 Three Phases of the Ring

A. First Phase   B. Second Phase   C. Third Phase

The ring is another expression of the bone stroke and is designed to train an artist to use reverse energy to bring out the vitality of a movement. The ring also helps the artist develop sensitivity to the tip of the brush, as well as to learn how to conceal the tip when making an abrupt end to a stroke. When making a ring, be aware of the following points.

The ring should always be perpendicular to the trunk; it should not be tilted (Fig. 4-6A). The three phases overlap one another; in other words, the second phase goes back into the first, the third into the second. Do not show a "lightning strike" (Fig. 4-6B). Both ends of the ring should appear to go around the trunk to the other side. Do not tuck the ends back into the gap between the sections (Fig. 4-6C). Try not to overextend the length of the ring (Fig. 4-6D). Turn the brush tip dutifully by reversing it as explained. When the turns are not sharp, the result is a ribbon-like shape (Fig. 4-6E).

Fig. 4-6 Undesirable Rings

A. Ring Not Perpendicular to the Trunk   B. Lightning Strike

C. Ring Tucked into Gap   D. Ring Overextended   E. Ribbon-like Ring

The phrase Eye of the Dragonfly is used to describe the ring on slender trunks or larger branches. This stroke is an abbreviated version of the ring stroke, without showing the "leaping line" described earlier as the second phase (Fig. 4-7).

Fig. 4-7 Eye of the Dragonfly

Branches

Key Ideas

The stroke for the bamboo branch is a slender version of the bone stroke.

Preparation

Use the Idea (or Basic-Hard) brush. Prepare a puddle of medium-tone ink. After preparing the brush, dip the tip about 1/3 the length of the brush in the medium ink. Stroke the excess moisture off the body along the saucer. Make sure the tip is grouped into a fine tip.

Movement

Set the tip down with pressure. Move the brush with your arm and maintain the vertical position of the handle. Use a steady and continuous motion and keep the same width during the course of each stroke. End with pressure and lift by a slight backward motion. Sometimes the branch stroke starts with a slight "pulling-back" motion and then pushes forward. The root sections are the heaviest point of the branches and the branches progressively become more slender as they move away from the trunk.

The branches should be rooted at one point on each ring. Root the branch clusters by alternating them from side to side along the main trunk.

The movement of the branches can be led from outside in (toward the trunk) or from inside out (away from the trunk). Follow the check mark ∨ movement (Fig. 4-8A).

All the branches should be positioned so that they form narrow angles in relation to the main body. Keep the branch ends in close proximity to one another so that the leaves can be grouped into continuous patterns (Fig. 4-8).

To keep the composition tight and project depth use "crossing," leaving a slight space when crossing trunk or main branches (Fig. 4-8B). However, for minor twigs you do not necessarily need to leave spaces when crossing.

Twigs need not show section rings or other visible divisions, and branching can be made freely along any point of the twigs.

Fig. 4-8 Branch Cluster

Branches should be made by arm motion, holding the brush vertically during the movement. Carry the tip of the brush all the way to the end of the branch (Fig. 4-9A). Do not let go of the brush tip (Fig. 4-9B).

Fig. 4-9 Branch Stroke

A. Correct

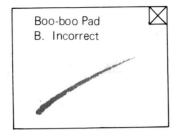

Boo-boo Pad
B. Incorrect

Turning should occur through additional branching (Fig. 4-10A). Do not turn the branch during a single stroke (Fig. 4-10B).

Fig. 4-10 Turning Branch

A. Turning through Branching

Boo-boo Pad
B. Wrong Turn

Always try to lead two lines together, then extend to join the third line (Fig. 4-11A). As with other forms, avoid the serious crime of chicken foot, where three similarly shaped lines cross or join at one point (Fig. 4-11B).

Fig. 4-11 Branch Joining

A. Better Branching

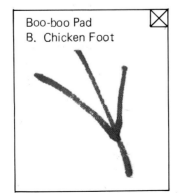

Boo-boo Pad
B. Chicken Foot

The flow of bamboo needs to be followed with ease. Branchings are done with the idea of Fishes Looking for the Same Food in mind. From each tip of the branch or twig, the fish should be able to swim effortlessly downstream to join the main body (Fig. 4-12A). Do not let your fish get lost in a maze (Fig. 4-12B).

Fig. 4-12 Branch Flow

A. Smooth Branching

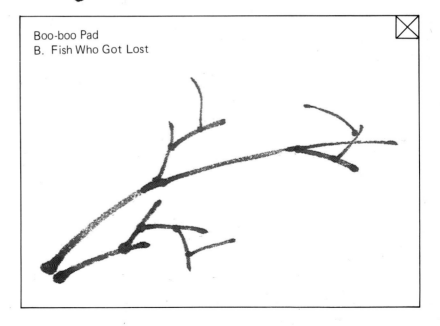

Boo-boo Pad
B. Fish Who Got Lost

Here are some branch groupings for your practice (Fig. 4-13).

Fig. 4-13 Branch Groupings

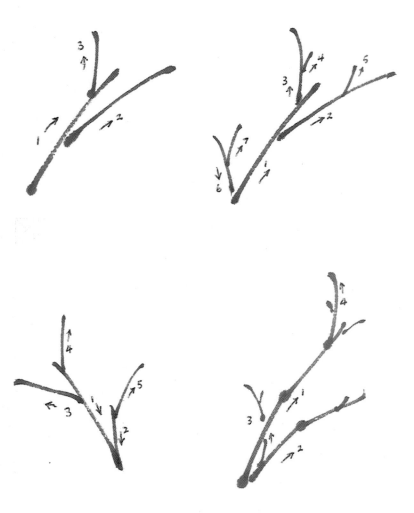

The Bone Stroke

General Discussion

Throughout this lesson, the term "bone stroke" has been brought up time and time again. What is the bone stroke anyway? If you do not feel curious by now, it's okay. You have already learned the essence of the spirit of the bone stroke.

In China, the orchid and bamboo are considered written, rather than painted, forms. The orchid is an exercise of the cursive "running" style of calligraphy. From our orchid lesson, we have seen how the natural movement of a brush stroke works. The orchid leaf is made by showing the natural trace of the brush tip.

The trunk, ring, and branch of the bamboo is a package study of the "regular" style of calligraphy. Chinese calligraphy requires squared shapes, and the bone stroke is the basis of such shapes.

The bone stroke is called "le 勒" in China. This character depicts the motion of halting a rapidly running horse by pulling back on its bit. The premise of the stroke is based on the idea that the energetic motion results when two opposing forces are at work. For instance, if we want to jump forward, we pull back to get ready. After jumping, we pull back to balance ourselves.

Besides capturing the vitality of an energetic motion, the bone stroke is also designed to conceal the tip of the brush at both ends of a stroke.

Method of the Bone Stroke

Use the Large Soft (or Basic-Soft) brush, well saturated with ink up to the halfway point. Hold the brush vertically and use your arm to move the brush at all times.

The Start

The start of the bone stroke is based on the statement "If one desires to go right, think left first." The start has three steps, as described below.

Land the tip, leading it slightly toward the upper left (Fig. 4-14A). Press down, allowing less than 1/4 of the length of the bristle to bend (Fig. 4-14B). The tip should stay put; do not let it travel down. (This is like the pivot foot, if you are a basketball fan, though most of you are probably not.) Swing the brush handle a 1/4 counterclockwise turn, with the pressure intact (Fig. 4-14C).

Fig. 4-14 The Start of the Bone Stroke

A. Landing the Tip   B. Pressing Down   C. The Swing

The result of these three steps is that the bending portion of the brush is now pointing to the left, the tip is spread and covering the entire width, and the left side is squared. In some cases the first step can be omitted. Try beginning by pressing down, then swinging the brush handle. This method should be easier.

The Cross

Now slightly let go of the pressure and forcefully push to the other side with arm movement. The most common mistake is starting the motion too soon, when the tip has not completed its turn. The result is that the tip moves along the topside of the stroke rather than being spread evenly in the center. The artist loses control.

The End

Mei Lan-kung, the Sung dynasty calligrapher, stated that "for every push forward, a retreating backward motion is there at the end."

After the cross movement, exert a little more pressure, then lift by letting the tip move slightly to the upper right. Finally, cut down to the lower right and end by reversing the tip backward (Fig. 4-15).

Fig. 4-15 Completed Bone Stroke

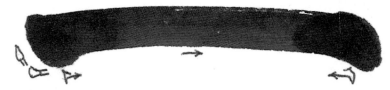

Try the bone stroke in the following ways: from top to bottom in this angle (Fig. 4-16A), and from bottom to top in this angle (Fig. 4-16B).

Fig. 4-16 Vertical Bone Strokes

A. From Top to Bottom   B. From Bottom to Top

In my many years of teaching, the praises greatly outweigh the complaints. One of the complaints, however, has been, "Now he tells us!" As if I liked to see my students suffer. Although I am a gentle person, this remark does irritate me. The reason for me to save the discussion of the bone stroke to the last is fairly obvious. I teach most of the time in Southern California, and there are a multitude of distractions. If I told my students that we were going to do bamboo painting and then started them through a series of torturous dog bones, when the next lesson came around I probably would find them next door taking belly dancing instead.

Now that I have worked up some real anger, let us do some bamboo leaves.

General Discussion

Many artists in China have spent their entire careers painting bamboo. The bamboo is generally regarded as one of the ultimate subjects for revealing the artistic as well as the spiritual nature of an artist. Many artists also consider bamboo one of the most difficult subjects and the bamboo leaves the toughest element to master. Do not let these artists scare you. Bamboo painting really is "a piece of cake."

The secret of painting bamboo is to have the leaf images in your heart. All the other elements — the trunk, the branches, the rings — are designed to reveal the leaves.

In bamboo painting, the leaves are rarely alone, as they enjoy the company of one another. In the "rainy-day bamboo," the leaves are clustered into "fan" shapes. A settling balance prevails which projects a feeling of tranquility.

Lesson 5
Bamboo, Part 2:
Leaves

Step-by-step Instruction

The Basic Leaf Stroke

Key Ideas

The stroke should be decisive and forceful, linking the movement into a dynamic rhythm. The stroke always moves from the stem, or root of the leaf, to its tip.

The vertical position of the brush must be maintained throughout the movement. Use more arm movement and less finger movement.

Land the stroke heavily and relax the pressure by lifting. Paint with one continuous motion; do not break the motion into two phases. The leaf shape should be wider at the start, with a more slender body at the tip.

Preparation

You can use the Idea (or the Basic-Hard) or the Big Idea brush. However, the very best brush for painting bamboo is the Orchid Bamboo. Make sure the brush tip is formed. Prepare 4-5 teaspoons of dark ink.

Loading the Brush

After a fine tip is formed, dip the tip 1/3 into water, release the excess moisture, then soak 1/2 the length of the brush in dark ink. The brush should look fat. If you see the tip is not pointed due to this fatness, do not worry; as long as all the bristles are straight, the brush will bounce back to a fine point.

Movement

Land the brush with pressure while at the same time starting the lifting motion. Notice the word "while." It is important to consider the landing and lifting as one movement. Keep the brush tip in the middle of the stroke (Fig. 5-1).

Fig. 5-1 Basic Leaf Stroke

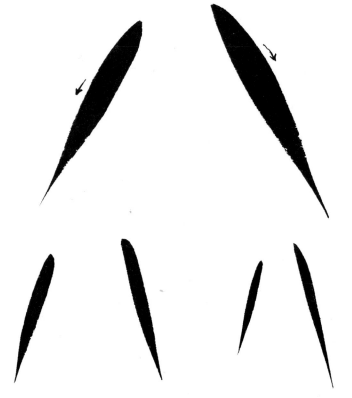

Some common problems with the leaf stroke (Fig. 5-2) are shown below:

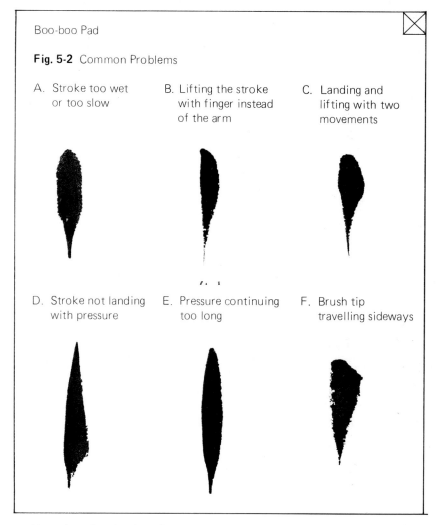

Boo-boo Pad

Fig. 5-2 Common Problems

A. Stroke too wet or too slow

B. Lifting the stroke with finger instead of the arm

C. Landing and lifting with two movements

D. Stroke not landing with pressure

E. Pressure continuing too long

F. Brush tip travelling sideways

Note that the tip should travel through the middle of every stroke. Do not land the tip sideways. Before starting the stroke, bend the brush bristles slightly to position the brush tip point opposite the direction of the stroke. Make sure the brush tip lands smoothly. When the direction of the leaves changes, the brush tip direction should be adjusted accordingly. Now do the following exercise as illustrated (Fig. 5-3).

Fig. 5-3 Brush Tip Staying in the Middle

Leaf in Profile

All the rainy-day bamboo leaves droop downward. The leaf bends, with the stem usually hiding in the back of the leaf. In some cases, though, the drooping leaf which is positioned at an angle needs to show its stem (Fig. 5-4).

Fig. 5-4 Drooping Leaves

Begin the stem with a thin bone stroke, let the brush tip complete its turn, then exert a little pressure while lifting it up (Fig. 5-5).

Fig. 5-5 Rainy-Day Leaf and Stem

The Leaf Grouping

Two Leaves

One host at the tip of the branch carries and extends the flow of the branch. One guest starts a little behind and is smaller. These are young leaves and, when they are shown in profile, they should be slender (Fig. 5-6).

Fig. 5-6 Host and Guest Leaf Grouping

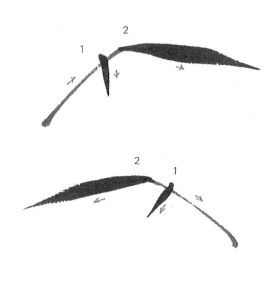

Certain host and guest formations should be avoided, as they will spoil the composition. Do not let the guest root too closely to or be too much the same size as the host (Fig. 5-7A). Do not let the guest become larger than the host (Fig. 5-7B). Do not leave too big a gap between the two leaves (Fig. 5-7C). Do not split the angle too far (Fig. 5-7D). Make sure the host leaf carries the flow of the branch and extends outward.

Do not let it turn and droop at the end (Fig. 5-7E). Think of the grandfather and father who worked very hard to send the son to college: Do not let the kid turn into a bum.

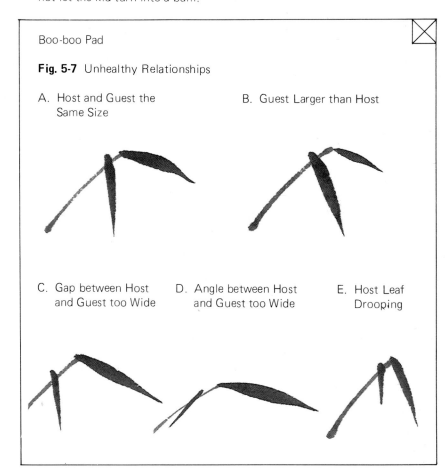

Boo-boo Pad

Fig. 5-7 Unhealthy Relationships

A. Host and Guest the Same Size

B. Guest Larger than Host

C. Gap between Host and Guest too Wide

D. Angle between Host and Guest too Wide

E. Host Leaf Drooping

Three Leaves

For this composition, paint the center leaf first, then the left and right leaves. This is the beginning of a fan shape (Fig. 5-8), and no matter how many more leaves are added the overall shape still is a fan (Fig. 5-8). For the younger generation, I have discovered the symbol for Batman (⋀⋀) to be an excellent pattern for the bamboo cluster.

Fig. 5-8 Fans

The leaves can overlap, but each has its own stem. Do not let them appear to be all growing from one stem (Fig. 5-9).

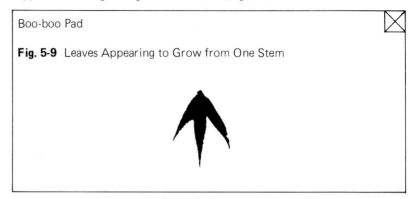

Boo-boo Pad

Fig. 5-9 Leaves Appearing to Grow from One Stem

The Fishes-Looking-for-the-Same-Food principle explained in Lesson Two still applies, with a slight modification. Here there are several sources of food, but they are close to one another, hiding below the root of the center leaf and along the tip of a twig (Fig. 5-10).

Fig. 5-10 Fishes Looking for the Same Food

Notice that the host, or center leaf, is slightly larger than the side leaves. Usually it is also rooted slightly higher. The host establishes the direction of the cluster.

The guests, or side leaves, should extend cheerfully outward instead of drooping down into a depressing shape (Fig. 5-11A). The tips of the side leaves should curve slightly toward the center leaf. Do not let them curve outward (Fig. 5-11B).

Also, do not let guests climb all over the host (Fig. 5-11C) or become totally dependent on the host (Fig. 5-11D).

Fig. 5-11 Undesirable Clusters

A. Side Leaves Depressed

B. Side Leaves "Gone Bananas

C. Guests Climbing
over the Host

D. Guests Dependent on Host

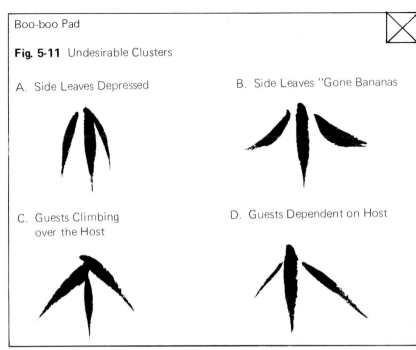

If the direction of the cluster favors one side, modify the attitude of each leaf and maintain a level top line. If the center leaf turns to the right, extend the right side leaf and widen its angle; meanwhile, shorten the left side leaf and narrow its angle to the center leaf (Fig. 5-12A). Do not simply turn the cluster without adjusting the positions of the leaves (Fig. 5-12B).

Fig. 5-12 Directional Adjustment

A. Cluster with Leaves
Modified toward Right

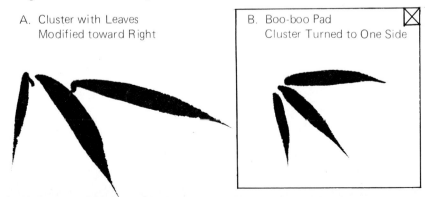

Four Leaves

In this composition the two center leaves serve as cohosts and act jointly to give direction to the whole group (Fig. 5-13A). Do not split these cohosts open too much (Fig. 5-13B).

Fig. 5-13 Four Leaves

A. Center Leaves as Cohosts

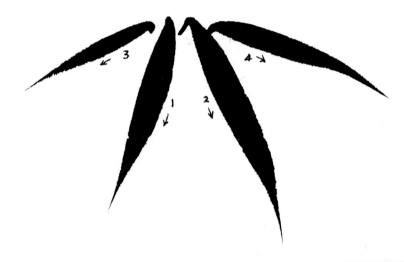

B. Cohosts Split Too Widely

If the center leaves do happen to split open, the side leaves should arch and extend to balance the composition. To avoid congestion, root the side leaves somewhat higher than and at a slight distance from the center leaves. In Chinese, the shape is referred to as the "frightened bird" (Fig. 5-14).

Fig. 5-14 Frightened Bird Four-Leaf Cluster

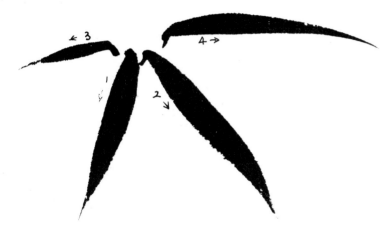

Five Leaves

The formation of the five-leaf cluster is similar to the frightened bird, but with smaller side leaves. The shape is called the "flying swallow" (Fig. 5-15).

Fig. 5-15 Flying Swallow

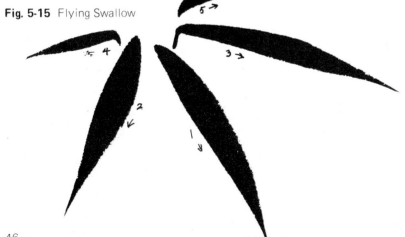

Crossing

Crossing the leaves helps develop depth, add variety, and extend the overall image of the cluster. If the number of leaves in a cluster exceeds five, two or more clusters are needed. Develop three or four leaves in one cluster. Then cross another cluster along the same level to build a new fan (Fig. 5-16).

Fig. 5-16 Crossing Leaves

Use a short leaf to cross a long leaf in order to keep the perimeter of the fan intact (Fig. 5-17A). Try not to use the long leaf to cross a short leaf (Fig. 5-17B).

Fig. 5-17 Attention to Fan

A. Fan Shape Intact

Boo-boo Pad
B. Fan Shape Crooked

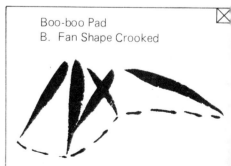

Do not let a member leaf of one group join another group and abandon its own "partner" (Fig. 5-18)

Boo-boo Pad

Fig. 5-18 Leaf Abandoning Its Partner

New Leaves

New leaves are unaware of the rainy conditions they will face. Unlike mature leaves which learn to compromise by drooping, new leaves shoot upward every which way they please. Usually two to three are in a cluster, and they uplift the spirit of the whole group and direct one group to meet another. In general, they add a great deal of cheerfulness to the composition.

Alternate the new leaves along a new twig of the branch (Fig. 5-19A). Do not let them tie into one point (Fig. 5-19B).

Fig. 5-19 New Leaves

A. New Leaves Alternating along Twig

Boo-boo Pad
B. New Leaves Tied into
   One Point of Twig

Since the new leaves come out wrapped like the shape of a needle, then open up, paint their roots narrower than the rest of the leaf. Link them onto the branch with a stem or suggest the stem by allowing a little distance between the twig and the leaf (Fig. 5-20).

Fig. 5-20 New Leaves Positioned on Twig

Leaves and Branches

Key Ideas

Most of the twigs shoot upward from a branch; it is the rainy condition which causes the leaves to droop. It is very important to have this mental picture in mind. Make sure the flow of all the branches and twigs can be carried smoothly and extended by the leaves. For drooping leaves, it is essential to turn the branch tip a little to prepare the leaves to turn downward (Fig. 5-21A). In order to develop the correct drooping tendency, the leaf clusters should be rooted higher than the branch and with enough distance between them to project a comfortable turn downward. Suggestion: Follow the tip of the twig upward a little; land the root of the host leaf above the tip of the twig, overlapping it with the tip of the twig; then let the side leaf extend along the flow of the twig (Fig. 5-21B). The leaves should not come out below the branch (Fig. 5-21C), nor should the stems show on top of the leaves (Fig. 5-21D). A rigid upright branch with leaves pointing straight down would look rather awkward. It reminds me of seeing my skinny, bald-headed uncle wearing a toupee at his wedding (Fig. 5-21E).

Fig. 5-21 Relationship of Leaves and Twigs

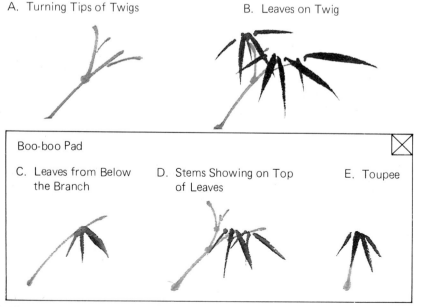

A. Turning Tips of Twigs

B. Leaves on Twig

Boo-boo Pad

C. Leaves from Below
   the Branch

D. Stems Showing on Top
   of Leaves

E. Toupee

Leaves and Trunk

The host leaf leads each of the clusters to radiate outward from the trunk. In each of the leaf groupings, leaves also should radiate from the center (Fig. 5-22).

Leaf Cluster Groupings

According to whether they are in light or shadow, young or old, showing the topside or the underside, in the front or in the back, the leaf clusters vary in shading from light to dark. It is important to present the vitality of yin and yang by showing extreme contrast, and it is also important to show, through stages, a smooth transition.

Start with the darkest leaf cluster and extend the movement with lighter clusters by gradually reducing the ink and adding water at the tip of the brush. Do not be concerned with a slight running or bleeding between the dark and light leaves, as it actually helps to blend the two shades (Fig. 5-23A). Do not show extreme dark or light without a happy medium in between (Fig. 5-23B).

Contrast among diversities is not limited to dark and light. Consider the contrast between large and small, thick and thin, space and painted forms. All diversities need to be presented in harmony.

Fig. 5-22 Leaf and Trunk Composition

Fig. 5-23 Different Shades of Leaves

A. Harmonious Transition of Contrast

Boo-boo Pad
B. No Happy Medium

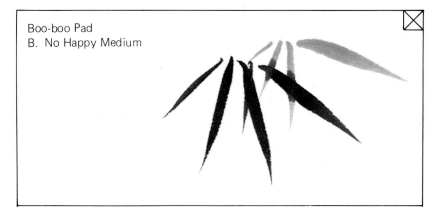

One Group

Arch open the wing leaves to display a cheerful outlook and maintain a level balance on top. Favor the angle of the branch, allowing the wing leaf to carry the flow of the branch (Fig. 5-24A).

Two Groups

The host group should be clustered in front and darker in tone than the guest. The guest should overlap, with its large leaf carrying the flow of the branch (Fig. 5-24B).

Three Groups

The first two groups form the host and the third group reaches to the back side. To convey depth, show the color of the third group lighter than the branch. The top group has arching wing leaves to uplift the spirit of the whole composition (Fig. 5-24C).

Four or More Groups

Project an overall "diamond" or "kite" shape to the branch cluster. Use the teamwork idea to develop forward, center, and guard units (Lesson Three), and maintain the host and guest relationships (Fig. 5-24D).

Fig. 5-24 Leaf Groupings

A. One Group   B. Two Groups

C. Three Groups   D. Four Groups

Conclusion

The bamboo leaf cluster is developed with a rhythmic movement, moving from the center leaf to the left leaf and then to the right and gradually extending outward. It never is a good idea to insert one leaf into an existing cluster, since the rhythm is not continuous. Should you wish to add more leaves, develop a new cluster.

All the clusters are relatively level along the top. The wing leaves on both sides are relatively balanced under normal conditions; however, should the center leaf turn to an angle, the wing leaves need to enhance the direction of the center leaf and eventually provide a settled feeling for the whole cluster. When the clusters extend, the shape may enlarge, but the basic fan shape remains and all the other considerations are the same.

In the next lesson, we will consider the role that leaf clusters play in overall bamboo composition.

Lesson 6
Bamboo, Part 3:
Composition

Introduction

The composition of bamboo includes all the important considerations in Chinese brush painting. The balance between contrasts, the relationship between host and guests, the design of the flow and movement, the distribution of space, the projection of depth, and the perimeter points of interest are all embraced in the study of bamboo.

Step-by-step Instruction

Preparation

Use a sheet of Double Shuen rice paper and lay the paper horizontally.

Use the Basic-Soft or the Large Soft brush for the trunks; use the Idea or the Basic-Hard brush for the rings, branches, and leaves.

Prepare dark ink and slightly tilt the ink slate or saucer for trunks and leaves. Prepare a small puddle of medium-toned ink in a separate saucer for branches.

The Trunks and Major Branches

Paint the host trunk, developing it at about the one-third point to the left of the paper and slightly angled to avoid straight up-and-down movement. Shape the spaces into a host-and-guest relationship.

Paint the guest trunk, making sure that the rings of the two trunks do not line up at the same levels. Make the guest trunk narrower and lighter than the host. To achieve unity between the trunks, use the Fishes-Looking-for-the-Same-Food principle to guide the guest to join the root of the host (Fig. 6-1A).

Now treat the above two trunks as the new host and draw a large branch as the guest. The branch should be rooted at a somewhat wide distance from the two trunks to develop a solid foundation. If the branch is too close to the trunks, the composition will lose its stability. Aim the root of the major branch more vertically than the trunks to avoid crashing into the trunks. Let the branch end with ample space in front of it so that its leaves will have room to extend (Fig. 6-1B).

Add the rings on the trunks and the eyes of the dragonfly on the branch. Do these while the trunks and the branch are still wet.

The Branches and Twigs

Host Group

Develop one cluster of branches on the upper left side of the host trunk and one cluster on the upper right side of the guest trunk. These two clusters form an "umbrella." Since the trunk frequently extends into the top of the paper, leading the viewer off the painting, the umbrella-styled cluster on the top area of the trunk is designed to guide the flow of the painting back to the center and split the trunk flow into two U-turns to bring it back (Fig. 6-1C).

Below the umbrella, develop the host cluster, which serves as the focus of this composition (Fig. 6-1D).

Guest Group

Develop two branch clusters alternating from the top sections of the major branch. The top cluster crosses the major branch to suggest that it is in front of the branch. The lower cluster bypasses the major branch, suggesting that it is behind the major branch.

The guest group helps to extend the dominant flow of the composition. However, you should also make an effort to bring the viewer's attention back to the host (Fig. 6-1E).

Liaison Group

Develop a liaison cluster between the host and guest group. The liaison forms the low point of a triangle, with the umbrella as the top point and the guest group as the side point. The focus is found inside this triangle. Make sure the liaison cluster is high enough so that its leaves will not go off the painting (Fig. 6-1F).

To balance the weight distribution, add one more branch cluster on the lower left area of the composition. Picture each trunk as the axis of a scale and be sure that the weight of the branch clusters is well distributed (Fig. 6-1G).

The weight of distribution and the direction of the branch clusters should be offset both from front and back and from side to side. Balance promotes stability, not sameness.

Examine the locations of the branch clusters. Make sure they do not line up vertically or horizontally. It is very easy to lengthen some branches or to expand the clusters by adding more branches. Try to develop the clusters with variation in mind (Fig. 6-2).

Fig. 6-1 Trunk and Branch Composition Diagram

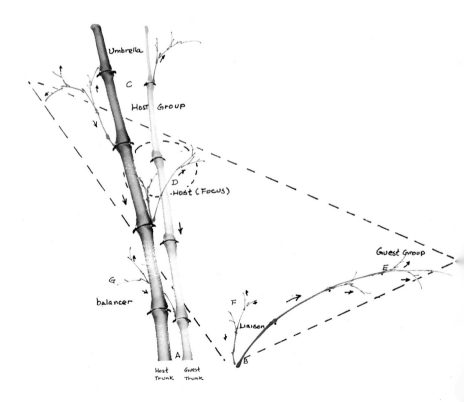

Fig. 6 2 Trunk and Branch Composition

53

Leaves

The Focus

Make the center leaf cluster of the host branches, then add an overlapping cluster to the right. Make sure the side leaf carries the flow of the branch. (This consideration should be kept in mind for all the leaf clusters.) Then develop one leaf cluster to the left of the center leaf cluster and one above it.

Each cluster should radiate outward from the center with balance between the left and the right sides, especially the far-reaching leaves on both sides of the whole group. Show clusters reaching both the front and the back sides of the twigs. The front-reaching clusters should be dark, and the back ones lighter than the twigs. The lower ones should be drooping; the top clusters should have arms cheerfully extended (Fig. 6-3A).

The Umbrella

Develop the dark leaves on the host (darker) trunk and the lighter leaves on the guest (lighter) trunk.

It is important to show leaves going both to the front and the back of the trunk to develop the dimensional quality of the composition. Do not paint light leaves on top of the dark trunk. Leaves need to be dark to cover the trunk and show they are in front of it. Lighter leaves should leap over the trunk to suggest they are behind it (Fig. 6-3B).

Guest Group

Paint the top cluster with dark leaves. Allow the right side leaf to fully extend the flow of the branch, but also try to use the left side leaf to lead the viewer's attention back to the host. Successful composition allows the viewer's attention to be led to the focal area of the painting. The focal area has a dominant host, and it should be enhanced by the flow of the perimeter points.

Develop the lower cluster with lighter leaves. Again make these leaves lighter than the branch to show that they are reaching to the back.

Note the gradual change between dark and light clusters. Rather than clear-cut contrast, the light and dark leaves are presented in harmonious ttransition (Fig. 6-3C).

Liaison Group

Develop one dark leaf cluster and one medium cluster.

The previous clusters all have penetrating points which favor one side in order to spearhead a movement into a wide open area of space. The centrally located liaison group is done with a different approach. Split the movement of the branch by using two leading points on both sides of the tip. The direction of the leaf clusters remains neutral (Fig. 6-3D).

Use the light tone for the lower left leaf cluster, thus making it less important so that it does not take attention away from the dominating tendency (Figs. 6-3E, 6-4).

Fig. 6-3 Leaf Composition Diagram

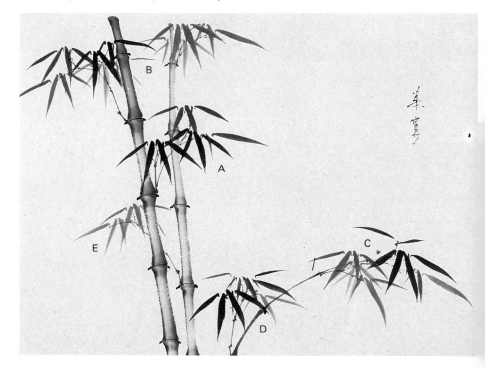

Fig. 6-4 Leaf Composition

Additional Comments

Each leaf cluster can display a balanced fan shape by having the top area relatively level and the two wing leaves extending out in a balanced formation. Consider each fan shape part of a group of pictures on the wall: If one frame goes crooked, it disturbs the whole wall (Fig. 6-5A). In this case, you can use one leaf cluster to adjust the balance of another. One way of doing this is to add one cluster to another by crossing. The result is a new fan shape (Fig. 6-5B).

Fig. 6-5 Balance within Leaf Cluster

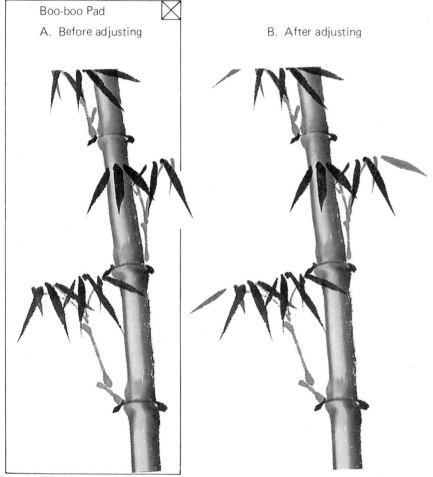

Boo-boo Pad

A. Before adjusting

B. After adjusting

I suspect that, in many cases, if one crooked leaf cluster is a mistake, then with two or three crooked ones, critics might begin to notice "a trend of style." In Chinese painting, we cannot go over a stroke to change it. If you make a "boo-boo," why not try doing a few more? Make them host "boos" and guest "boos." Variety is important (Fig. 6-6).

Fig. 6-6 Host Boo and Guest Boo

To summarize, successful bamboo composition has leading points which extend in various directions. These points are the spearheads of the different directional flows and should have no competitive points alongside them to weaken their importance. These points divide the space around the bamboo into distinguishable areas, directing and extending the flow into the open areas or linking these areas back to the focal area of the painting. They highlight the various shapes.

Do not allow three or more perimeter points to form one continuous line (Fig. 6-7A). Usually, it is best to allow the shortest point to be in the middle of two longer ones. The space is then shaped into a "V," which immediately leads the viewer to the center of the painting. Picture the relationship of shape and space to one of "water to land." To make the land more beautiful, we have rocky coastlines, gulfs, peninsulas, islands, streams and lakes (Fig. 6-7B).

Fig. 6-7 Perimeter Arrangements

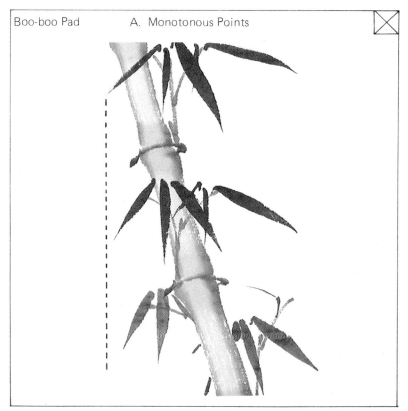

Boo-boo Pad   A. Monotonous Points

B. "V" Space

Be sensitive to presenting all the elements with variation. Avoid parallel formation of the trunks and branches, identical levels between the rings of the trunks, or lining up the leaf clusters horizontally or vertically.

大 熊 貓

Fig. 7-1

Da	Hsiung	Mao
(Big)	(Bear)	(Cat)

Lesson 7

Panda

The Idea of Panda

This lesson is designed to reward the artists who have just completed the basic line work training through the orchid and bamboo studies. By studying the panda, we can now change the all-too-serious artistic mood into a delightful, casual pursuit of fun — which is why most of us paint to begin with.

Because it uses a minimum of shapes and lines, the panda exercise will help to "turn the artist loose." The cheerful dots and blending of ink in this exercise cleverly suggest a playful spirit. Through this exercise, many artists discover the true meaning of spontaneity.

No animal, not even the imaginary dragon, has enjoyed such enormous popularity in the past decade as the panda. The stuffed-animal-like creature has an irresistible, winning personality which charms the spirit of the child in all of us.

The panda is found only in China. Apart from its rarity, the panda has an exquisite form, with starkly contrasting black-and-white fur. Bamboo is its main diet and often serves as an accent to a panda painting. All these qualities make the panda a very desirable brush painting subject.

Although the panda has moments of losing its cool, especially when the Japanese zookeeper decides to conduct those untimely matchmaking sessions, it is generally considered a peace-loving animal. Its every act —

sitting, climbing, reclining, gazing, rolling — demonstrates its playful attitude. Every pose is entertaining and inspirational to a throw-ink brush painter.

The panda has no predators. Although it appears awkward, it can turn and flee in the twinkling of an eye, climbing up a tall pine with surprising agility or swimming across a river. Its size and powerful claws also are duly noticed by the common predators, and most animals tend to leave pandas alone.

The panda can mate and have babies when it is three or four years old. If it stays healthy, it can live as long as thirty years.

The panda has a special weakness for water, as some people do with wine. When pandas come to the stream, they drink until their stomachs can hold no more. Many times they are found unconscious by the stream from overdrinking.

The home of the panda is destined to become China's most beautiful national park. High above the Szechwan Basin, on top of the Min Mountains at altitudes from five to ten thousand feet, the Min River cascading through dense bamboo forests — here is where the main concentration of pandas live. Eventually, the Min River comes down to the densely populated Ching-do Plain, irrigating thousands of acres of fertile land and finally joining forces with the mighty Yangtze River. But high above the plain and far away from the madding crowd, the panda prefers to live a solitary life. No one knows how many are there.

I do want to mention the beauty of one area where the panda is found: Chiu Sai Kou (九寨溝, Nine Fort Waterway). Hundreds of jade blue lakes lie along this river valley, which is surrounded by snow-capped mountains. Petrified woods in splendid colors rest at the bottom of these lakes, and the water is so transparent that all colors and varieties of water plants are clearly visible. These lakes are located on different levels and are connected by hundreds of waterfalls. When autumn comes, the whole valley turns into different colors; with the blue sky, snow-covered mountains, and cascading waters, it is indeed the "Land of the Fairies."

And people wonder why the pandas do not want to make babies at the zoo!

China's changing attitude toward the West in recent years, especially through the effort of Prime Minister Dung Hsiung-ping, has made the panda a symbol of goodwill. Since Dung is from Szechwan, and he himself looks like a panda, what better image can the new China seek?

The Anatomy of the Panda

The panda is called a bear because of its size and its heavy limbs; however, zoologists place it in the raccoon family. To Chinese people, the panda is the panda.

The panda is heavy-bodied, grows up to six feet in height and weighs about 250 to 300 pounds. Compared to a bear, the panda's head is rounder and its nose and lips shorter. It has a very short tail (about eight inches).

The face of the panda is incredibly cute. The eyes are encircled by tilted black patches located closely beside a large white nose. At the underside of the nose, near the nostrils, is a black triangle. The forehead takes up one-half the length of the face (to the Chinese, the length of one's forehead indicates one's intelligence). At the top of the head stands a pair of dark "Mickey Mouse" ears.

The body of the panda is black and white in sharply demarcated areas. The legs are black. The black of the front legs continues up over the shoulders and provides a strip of dark arches across the back. Some of the dark hair on the front legs reaches into the chest area, and the rest of the body is white. The panda has long and sturdy claws which can carry the weight of the whole body when climbing trees (Fig. 7-2).

Fig. 7-2 Pandas

Materials and Preparation

Use the Idea or the Basic-Hard brush for the lines and the Flower and Bird or the Basic-Comb brush for the ink shades.

For best results, use the Flow brush for the lines and Large Flow brush for the ink shades.

Pre-mix a medium-toned ink on the saucer (about 2 teaspoonfuls). Prepare about 5 teaspoonfuls of dark ink.

Use Double Shuen rice paper.

Wet the vermillion with 2 to 3 drops of water to soften the chips.

We will begin our full-color exercises after the panda lesson. Please acquire the necessary Chinese colors and prepare them according to the instructions given in Lesson One.

Step-by-step Instruction

Head

Key Ideas

The shape of the panda's head resembles a spade in a deck of playing cards (Fig. 7-3A); in profile, it looks like a pear (Fig. 7-3B). Make the face wider than the length to show a more delightful quality.

Fig. 7-3 Head

A. Front View

B. Profile

As mentioned before, the forehead takes up one-half the length of the face, and the eyes, nose, and mouth are squeezed in the middle area just below the forehead.

In front view, the face features can be divided as shown in Figure 7-4. In profile, the eye patch is approximately at the area shown in Figure 7-5.

Fig. 7-4 Feature Proportions: Front View

Fig. 7-5 Feature Proportions: Profile

The line work is loose and carefree, with variations in the width of the lines. The lines are not tightly connected, in order to give more of a spirit of freedom.

All the ink dots are done with a delightful "bounce."

Method

Line Work

Use the Idea, Basic-Hard, or the Flow brush, form the tip, and load the tip with medium ink up to 1/5 length. Keep the bristle body dry. Hold the brush vertically at all times.

In the front view, the procedure is as indicated in Figure 7-6A. Note that the head is balanced on both sides, and the nose lines are relatively parallel to the sides of the face.

In the profile, the procedure is as indicated in Figure 7-6B. Use two strokes for the forehead; however, do not make the forehead too pointed.

Fig. 7-6 Stroke Sequence for Panda Head

A. Front View   B. Profile

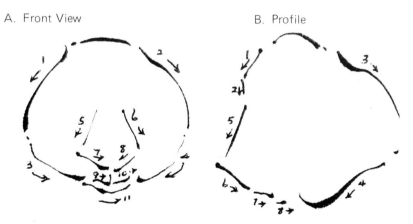

Curve the side lines of the face outward instead of downward to insure the proper width of the face. A space may show between the side of the face and the cheek lines to make the turn softer. Curve the cheek line more horizontally and make the face line longer than the cheek line. Sometimes, using a dot between lines can soften the turn, add freedom of motion, but still suggest continuity.

Begin the nose line a little above the midpoint of the length of the face. For the front view of the head, estimate 1/5 the width of the face for the upper width of the nose, then draw two lines downward for the side of the nose. The lines for the lower part of the nose can begin with a soft turn to soften the shape of the nose. For the profile of the head, use three lines to form the nose. The first line is the longest; the second line is more flexible and ends near the level of the cheek line. Turn to add the third line. Add the lip line or show the whole mouth; then add the top line of the face (Fig. 7-7).

Fig. 7-7 Nose, Mouth, and Forehead

Ink Work

Use the Flower and Bird, the Basic-Comb, or the Large Flow brush. After the tip is formed, dip the tip 1/6 its length into water and stroke off the excess moisture on the bristle body. Dip the tip 1/4 length with the dark ink and spread the tip a little.

Eye patches: Exert a slight pressure at the top and increase pressure at the end. The eye patches tilt downward and outward from the ridge of the nose lines, curving inward like the top half of parentheses (Fig. 7-8A). If you'd like to show the tiny little eyes of this lovely creature, use one large stroke with a small stroke encircling a small space to suggest the eye. To soften the edges of the shape, you can rinse the ink off the brush and wipe off the moisture, then use the clean brush to accent around the eye. This technique is called "breaking the ink." It must be done while the ink is still wet. I usually run the clear brush along the top edge of the eye patches, much like a lady applying eyeliner. Then, I use two or three dots to tilt the outside corner of the eye patches upward to give somewhat of a "Cleopatra" look to this lovely creature (Fig. 7-8B).

Fig. 7-8

A. Eye Patches

B. Eye Patches with Eyes

In the front view of the panda, position the patches close to the outline of the nose; each should take up about 1/5 of the face width (Fig. 7-9A). In the profile view, locate the patches at about the 1/3 point of the width of the face and the 1/2 point of the length (Fig. 7-9B). Add a triangular-shaped dot just below the tip of the nose.

Fig. 7-9 Panda with Eye Patches

A. Front View   B. Profiles

To do the ears, hold the brush at a slightly oblique angle, work two parentheses-like strokes with pressure, and overlap these strokes. For right-handed painters, it is natural to draw the left side of the ear by holding the brush more vertically and to make a skinnier stroke. But then tilt the brush in a more oblique position to draw the right side of the ear with a much fatter stroke (Fig. 7-10).

Fig. 7-10 Ears

In the front view, separate the ears farther apart than the eye patches. Ears should be balanced with their roots coming into the top head line. After the ink strokes are done, rinse off the ink on the bristles, stroke off the moisture and split the bristle tip. Brush a couple of strokes under each ear to break its solid shape and make the root blend into the head more naturally (Fig. 7-11A). In the profile, the front ear can blend into the outline of the face. Treat the root of the front ear the same way as the ears of the front view. The back ear stays above the forehead line (Fig. 7-11B).

Fig. 7-11 Head with Ears

A. Front View

B. Profile

"Adding a touch of vermillion to show the tongue really brings out the clever spirit of the panda."

Body

Key Ideas

A baby panda's head is disproportionally large in relation to the body, about a one-to-two ratio. For a mature panda, the body can be three to five times the length of the head. In paintings, we try not to make the body too large (I try to make the body about 1-1/2 times the size of the head).

The back of the panda continues in a line from the top of the forehead, arching up at the shoulder area, then tapering downward. The black hair on the front legs extends into the shoulder, wraps around the back like an arch, and cuts the white body into two parts (Fig. 7-12).

Fig. 7-12 Panda, Full Body

Method

The lines are the same as the head lines in tone and spirit.

To do the ink work, form the brush tip, dip the tip 1/4 length in water, and saturate the tip 1/3 length in dark ink. Use one to three strokes to form the various shapes. Split the bristle tip slightly to prevent the shapes from becoming too pointed.

Make sure the strokes overlap and that the edges of the strokes are connected to present a smooth shape. Be sensitive about the shapes of the spaces around the strokes.

The Back Arch and the Front Legs

Do one stroke for the back arch (Fig. 7-13).

Fig. 7-13 Back Arch

The upper portion of the front leg consists of three strokes. The left side is the continuation of the arch stroke of the back. Then turn the brush to an oblique angle to do a center stroke. Turn the brush to a more oblique angle for the right side stroke of the upper arm and make its width slightly narrower than the head (Fig. 7-14).

Fig. 7-14 Upper Section of the Front Leg

The lower section of the leg consists of two embracing strokes. Do these strokes in the reverse direction to join them onto the upper portion of the leg. Make the lower section about the length of the head (Fig. 7-15).

Fig. 7-15 Lower Section of the Front Leg

Add two strokes for the paw (Fig. 7-16).

Fig. 7-16 Paw

The other front leg should project its connection to the other side of the back arch. Position the brush at an oblique angle to do one or two strokes (Fig. 7-17).

Fig. 7-17 Front Body of Panda

It is interesting to note the various possibilities for connecting the lower body to the upper body (Fig. 7-18).

Fig. 7-18 Different Positions Using the Same Upper Body

Back Legs

On the back portion of the panda body the dark hair is limited to the legs and the dark area is much shorter.

After loading the ink, dip the very tip of the brush into water to tone down the tip portion a little. The legs should appear to be integrated with the white space of the body. Use three strokes to complete the back legs (Fig. 7-19). Sometimes using a spray bottle filled with clear water can soften the ink work on the body of the panda. Spray with a fine mist right after the legs are done and the ink is still wet. Be careful not to spray the face of the panda, to avoid unnecessary bleeding on the rice paper.

Fig. 7-19 Completed Panda

Sitting Panda

The front view of a sitting panda has the following lines: The shape of the body frame is similar to that of the head, with its size about one and one-half times larger than the head. A square-shaped tail is at the base of the body. Show the chest and suggest the stomach, allowing the shoulders to follow the head lines. I like to turn the body at a slightly different angle to the head to generate a graceful flow (Fig. 7-20). Add the ink work as diagrammed in Figure 7-21.

Fig. 7-20 Line Work of Sitting Panda

69

Fig. 7-21 Pandas

Fig. 8-1

Shan
(Mountain)

Cha
(Tea)

Lesson 8
Camellia, Part 1:
Flowers

The Idea of Camellia

The camellia lessons provide a basic study of the key concepts in composing a "cup-shaped" flower and in the different strokes used to present the different attitudes of a leaf. We shall also study the relationship between the flower, the leaves, and the branches in order to put together a "masterpiece." I can always sense the joy of celebration in my beginners' classes when we complete the camellia studies. Every budding face tells me that they feel they have finally "arrived."

The camellia is the most popular and highly respected flower in southwest China. It was honored as the national flower for the ancient southern kingdom, Dai Li (today's Yunnan Province). In a land marked by steep hills and roaring rapids, in early spring the camellia transforms the hills and valleys into oceans of red and white.

The symmetrical beauty and long-lasting quality of this flower have long been appreciated by young lovers as tokens for expressing mutual devotion. In the eyes of the Chinese, the petals reflect the spirit of a lady, and the holder of the petals (the calyx) represents the young man entrusted by the lady to be her protector. When the camellia has finished blooming, the calyx falls from the branches with the petals (unlike with most other flowers, where the calyx seems to decide to hang around the tree even after the petals have dropped). This phenomenon symbolizes an everlasting union between lovers.

The Anatomy of the Camellia

The single-layered camellia is one of the most valued flowers in China. It is the flower we shall study.

Petals. Camellias usually have five petals, although some varieties have six. Each petal is round along the perimeter, with a slight indentation at the middle point. The color on the top of the petal is stronger than that on the underside.

Pistil. The pistil is long, it is positioned at the center of the flower, and its has an impressive stigma at its tip.

Stamens. The stamens encircle the pistil, stand vertically, and form a barrel shape. They are quite thick and give the flower a unique formation. Their roots are connected into one body.

Pollen. Pollen is formed as impressive dots at the tip of the stamens.

Calyx. Scale-like and layered, the calyx forms a socket under the petals to "house" the flower.

Leaves. The leaves are dark and sturdy and have a noticeable center vein.

Stem. The stem connects the leaf to the branch.

Branches. The branches are woody and sturdy (Fig. 8-2).

Materials and Preparation

Paper and Brushes

Use Double Shuen rice paper.
Use the Flower and Bird or Basic-Comb. brush for the petal and leaf.
Use Idea or Basic-Hard brush for the pistil, stamens, pollen, vein of the leaf, and branch.

For best results, use the Flower and Bird or Large Flow brush for the petal and leaf; the Flow, Idea, or Big Idea for the pistil, stamens, pollen; and vein; and the Orchid Bamboo brush for the branch.

Colors

Since this is the first full-color lesson in the series, please carefully review the general color information in Lesson One.

Chinese color chips (chunks) include: yellow, indigo, vermillion, burnt sienna, red.

For the Students' Set, use Guta watercolors and check Lesson One to find the appropriate substitution tubes for the Chinese color chips. OAS Artists' Poster White. Ink.

Color Preparation

Yellow: Divide the chunks into two containers; one yellow remains "clean"; the other is used to mix with indigo to produce green. From now on, we will call this second yellow "dirty yellow."

Wet each yellow with 1 teaspoon of water. Let the chunks soak for several minutes to soften the colors.

Indigo: Wet the chips with 2 to 3 drops of water.

Strong light green: When the above colors are softened, use a brush to bring some of each of the colors into a dish. Mix indigo and dirty yellow with a little water, using more dirty yellow and less indigo to make the green lighter. Keep this light green thick. It will be used for the calyx.

Diluted light green: Use the same ratio of indigo and dirty yellow as above, but with more water (about 2 teaspoons); make a puddle of this color on another dish.

Vermillion, burnt sienna, red: Wet each with 2 to 3 drops of water. Soften some of the vermillion and burnt sienna into a weak diluted shade. Keep the red strong and thick.

Keep the poster white in the jar. Add a few drops of water and stir it until it is creamy.

Prepare 1 teaspoon of dark ink.

Fig. 8-2 Elements in the Camellia

Color and Moisture Chart

Element	Moisture	Colors
petals underside topside center area	wet 1/3 dry	medium vermillion 1/3 medium vermillion 1/3 + strong red 1/4 topside colors + thick red 1/4
pistil/stamens	wet tip 1/4	creamy white 1/4
pollen	wet tip 1/4	thick yellow + creamy white
calyx	wet 1/3	strong light green 1/3 + thick red 1/8
leaf topside underside vein	wet 1/3 wet 1/3 dry	medium light green 1/2 + strong indigo 1/3; blend tip into dark green + thick indigo 1/6 (+ ink 1/6 if needed) medium light green 1/2 strong dark green + ink
branch	medium 1/6	diluted burnt sienna + ink, mix into diluted dark brown 1/4
tree dots	dry	thick dark ink

Again, the fractions above refer to the length of the brush hair from the tip upward. These are rough estimates to help students load colors on the brush; Chinese painting is not a science. I was shocked to see one student who brought in a ruler to measure the accuracy of her fractions. Please!

Loading Colors

The spontaneous blending of contrasting colors within one stroke is one of the most exciting qualities of brush painting. The following steps are crucial:

Load each color two to three times, each time stronger than before and at a shorter length than before so that variation can occur within each color.

After each loading, press the tip of the brush on the saucer and stir a little to mix the colors.

The first color (the base color) is usually the weakest and goes into the bristle at the deepest length. The successive colors (tip colors) are thicker and shorter on the bristle.

Color Degrees

The terms thick, strong, medium, and weak are used in describing the intensity of the colors. They can be tested as follows, using Chinese red as an example (Fig. 8-3):

Fig. 8-3

Thick	Strong	Medium	Weak

The best variation is achieved by using the bristle body, as well as the tip of the brush (by pressing and oblique positioning the bristle). If a stroke is done only with the tip, only the tip color will show, and then what on earth do we need to go through such an extensive loading process for?

In many cases, the painting is done with the tip half of the brush. If colors go beyond 1/2 length, most shapes will be hard-edged and rigid.

Step-by-step Instruction

Flower Petals

Key Ideas

The open flower is shown in an oval shape with two petals in the front and three in the back, or vice versa. The front petals are folded, i.e., their inside edges are connected into a U-curve to house the stamens and pistil (Fig. 8-4A). The profile of the flower forms a cup shape, with the underside of the petals in the front and the topside of the petals in the back. The baseline of the petals forms a U-curve (Fig. 8-4B).

Fig. 8-4 Basic Shapes

A. Oval Formation of the Open Camellia

B. Camellia Flowers in Profile

All the petals come toward the center, like Fishes Looking for the Same Food.

Method

Preparation

Use the Flower and Bird or Basic-Comb. brush, form the tip, and dip tip 1/3 into water. Stroke off the excess moisture.

Open Flower

Lower Petals

Load the bristle tip 1/3 length with strong vermillion; blend the tip a little to allow the vermillion to reach about 1/2 length. Load the tip several times with the vermillion. Then with the very tip (about 1/4) load strong red and blend the tip to soften the red.

I know in past lessons I have emphasized the merit of holding the brush vertically, but I will not in this case. Hold the brush at a 45-degree angle with the tip pointing to the right. Work two strokes to form the right-side petal.

Do the first stroke with the tip working in a curve like this ↗ , and the second stroke like this ↘ (Fig. 8-5).

Fig. 8-5 Right Side Petal

Do not make the two strokes like parentheses (), as this will not bring the petals to the center (Fig. 8-6A). Do not work the stroke too rigidly (Fig. 8-6B). If the shape is too narrow, you still are holding your brush too vertically. The variation of colors also requires more bristle body to be in contact with the paper (Fig. 8-6C).

Even if you are using some of the best brushes recommended for this course, the brushes still have limitations. When working at an oblique angle, do not allow more than 2/3 the bristle length to be in contact with the paper. If you force the whole bristle body to be in contact with the paper, you will lose control of the tip (Fig. 8-6D). Begin the second stroke at a distance from the start of the first stroke to show the petal folding (Fig. 8-6E).

Boo-boo Pad

Fig. 8-6

A. Petals like parentheses   B. Too rigid

C. Shape too narrow   D. Pressure too hard   E. Second stroke starting too close to the first

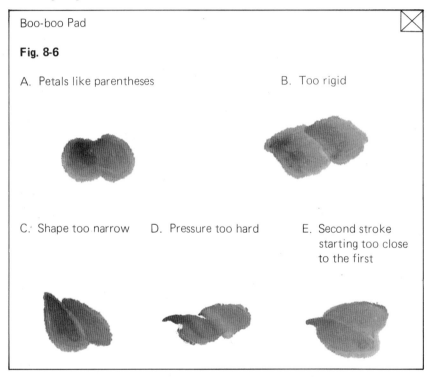

Now that you have done the right petal, the left-side petal should be a piece of cake — simply reverse everything! In reality, it is not so easy. To do the left side, first load the brush the same way that you did for the right side and hold the brush at an oblique angle. The tip now is pointing to the right. Do the right side of the left petal first, connecting the starting point with the existing petal (Fig. 8-7A). Then work the other side. When the two petals are completed, the top edge of the connected petals should form a U-shape (Fig. 8-7B). These petals do not need to be identical.

Fig. 8-7

A. Right Side of the Left Petal   B. Connected Petals Forming a "U"

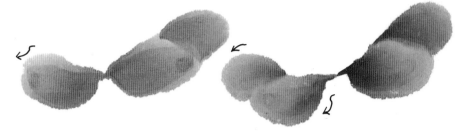

Common mistakes are found in the following illustrations: the two petals not connected (Fig. 8-8A); a flat top edge of the petals (Fig. 8-8B), or petals turning into a sharp "V" (Fig. 8-8C).

Boo-boo Pad

Fig. 8-8 Problems

A. Petals unconnected   B. Top edge too flat   C. Sharp "V"

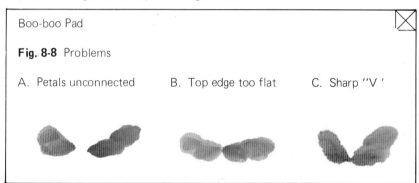

The U-shape can also be formed by three petals (Fig. 8-9).

Fig. 8-9 The Three Petals "U"

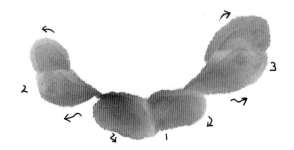

Top Petal

To do the left and the center top petals, work the strokes from the outside in. The wider petal can use up to three strokes. The right top petal can move from the center out. Leave space between the lower and top petals (Fig. 8-10). When doing the three strokes of the wider petal, think of the football player with tall shoulder pads. Do the left side of the petal with the brush held more vertically. Press down the tip, then spring with an arch to the left to show the shoulder pad. Then turn your brush more obliquely, with the tip pointing to the left, work a center stroke, and finally work a third stroke on the right. (Please watch the television demonstration carefully on the combination of these strokes.)

Fig. 8-10

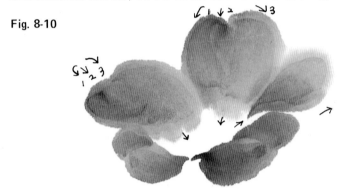

Do not turn the perimeter into a square (Fig. 8-11A). Extend the left- and right-side top petals beyond the two lower petals to form the oval shape (Fig. 8-11B). Try to estimate the room required for all three petals. If one petal takes up too much room (Fig. 8-11C), cut it short with the next petal (Fig. 8-11D).

Fig. 8-11 Problems of Top Petals and Remedies

Boo-boo Pad

A. Square

Remedy

B. Oval by extended
side petals

Boo-boo Pad

C. Petal too large

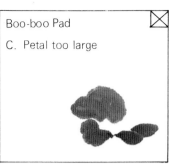

Remedy

D. Large petal cut
short by overlaid
petal

Center Area

Keep the brush bristle relatively dry. Load the vermillion and red as before and load the tip 1/6 length with thick red. Blend the tip to soften the color, but still keep the thick red strong. For these strokes, hold the brush vertically. The bristle tip can split a little. Set the pressure along the edge of the lower petals. Start from the center of the U-shape, move up by applying pressure down, and then work the strokes by blending upward into the wet petals on top (Fig. 8-12A). Overlap the center strokes and eventually fill the whole center area (Fig. 8-12B).

Fig. 8-12 Center Strokes

A. Stroke

B. Center Completed

Profile Flower

Underside

Load the bristle 1/3 with medium vermillion; blend to 1/2 length. Beginning with the middle petal, tilt the brush obliquely, and work with a motion like parentheses (). The side petals can be done with two movements each or one continuous motion. If you are having trouble regrouping the bristle at the end of the stroke, try using the Idea or Basic-Hard brush. To suggest depth, allow the side petals to start higher and end higher than the center petal. The underside forms a U-curve.

Topside

Work these petals by using the same method as used with the fully opened flower (Fig. 8-13).

Fig. 8-13 Profile Petals

Pistil and Stamens

Preparation

Mix white until it is creamy, thick but wet. Also mix thick yellow with the creamy white, using more white and less yellow. Use the creamy white for the stamens and the pistil. Use yellowish white for the pollen.

Pistil

Using the Idea or Basic-Hard brush, dip the tip 1/4 into water and load the creamy white generously at the tip several times. The white should be impressive, but not dry. Start from the tip of the pistil and split the oval shape in half with a bone line. (Exert slight pressure on both ends, maintain even pressure in the process, and keep the tip travelling in the middle.) Add a dot for the stigma at the tip. The root of the pistil should reach the center of the flower (Fig. 8-14A). Develop the length, allowing the top portion to curve slightly to show grace. Avoid having the pistil become too rigid. Do not curve the lower portion (Fig. 8-14B).

Fig. 8-14

A. Pistil

Boo-boo Pad

B. Pistil that missed the center

Stamens

The stamens are shorter than the pistil, and they form a barrel-like shape to encircle it. The top of the stamen curves inward to get the attention of the pistil; the lower portion stands vertically. Develop the lower layer very tightly with the roots connecting and with the center ones shorter and straighter. The side stamens should be taller and more curved (Fig. 8-15A). Add a few stamens as a top layer (Fig. 8-15B).

Fig. 8-15 Stamens

A. Front Layer

B. Barrel-Shaped Stamens

Pollen

Load the tip generously with yellowish-white. Drop the dots onto the top of each stamen with a scooping pressure (similar to the scoop motion used to serve ice cream). The pollen dots should be impressive and cute (Fig. 8-16).

Fig. 8-16 Pollen

Calyx

Use the Idea or Basic-Hard brush. Load strong light green about 1/3 length. Load the tip with thick red 1/8 length; blend the tip. Work the scales with overlapping strokes. Each stroke might need to be reloaded with red (Fig. 8-17).

Fig. 8-17 Calyx

Bud

The bud is usually darker than the flower. Although the petals show their underside, use the topside colors (vermillion with red). Use the Flower and Bird or Basic-Comb. brush and work the center front petal with two strokes. To work the side petals, begin on top of the center petal, move outward with pressure, then scoop the tail end inward to wrap around the center petal. Work the back petals sideways (Fig. 8-18).

After practicing the strokes for the three stages of camellia flowers — bud, profile, and fully opened — you can move on to the next lesson, which presents the leaves and branches (Fig. 8-19).

Fig. 8-18 Bud

Fig. 8-19 Camellia

Lesson 9
Camellia, Part 2:
Leaves and Branches

Introduction

So far in this series you have learned to paint two types of leaves: the orchid and the bamboo. Each of these leaves is made with one flowing stroke. The camellia leaf is more complex than either orchid or bamboo because it consists of several strokes and has several variations in shapes.

You will again pay an extensive visit to our old friend the bone stroke, in making the camellia branches. You will also be introduced to "happy dots." This lesson is a nice combination of the old and the new.

Step-by-step Instruction

Leaves

Key Ideas

Like the petals of the flower, the camellia leaves are short-stemmed. They have dentate, or tooth-like edges, which gives us an excuse not to have them perfectly smooth. They are a glossy, dark green color and are arranged alternately along the branches.

The stem of the leaf follows the tendency of the branch, which is usually upward. The leaves themselves may droop down as the result of weathering or the branch angle, but the stem always comes out from the branch in the angle favoring the direction of the branch. Do not let the stem bend downward from the branch.

To study a human figure, we need to know the bone structure. To study a leaf, we need to know the center vein. The center vein is the soul of the leaf. In order to make the leaf graceful, the center vein is projected as curved (Fig. 9-1) rather than as a straight line (Fig. 9-2). Every stroke must be made by thinking, "How does this stroke relate to the center vein?"

Fig. 9-1 Center Vein Curved

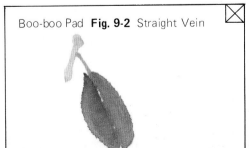

Boo-boo Pad **Fig. 9-2** Straight Vein

Preparation

Use the Flower and Bird or Basic-Comb. brush. Mix a puddle of medium-light green and a mixture of thick dark green by using dirty yellow and indigo. Soften the indigo chips with 2 to 3 drops of water, keeping the indigo thick. Prepare 2 teaspoons of ink.

Loading the Brush

Topside Leave

Dip 1/4 length of the bristle in water; stroke the excess off. Load 1/2 length with light green. Load the tip 1/3 length with thick, dark green and 1/4 with thick indigo and blend the tip area. Dip the tip 1/4 length in ink.

Underside Leaves

Dip 1/4 length in water. Load 1/2 light green, tip 1/4 dark green; blend the tip area.

Movement

Front View (Regular) Leaves

Leaves Facing the Right

.Of the two sections divided by the center vein, the left side is larger and wider, the right side smaller and narrower. To allow the stem to flow naturally downward into the branch, present the center vein in a curve (Fig. 9-3A).

To do the left side, tilt the brush tip to the left and exert pressure while letting the tip travel along the left side. Allow the bristle body to maintain a smooth curve on the right side to show the center vein. Learn to work the stroke by turning the handle of the brush. Start with the brush held more vertically, then tilt to scoop the tip outward (to the left) while exerting pressure. Gradually turn the handle vertically again, then lift the tip with a scoop to the right. Learn to end the movement to the right by relaxing pressure so you do not alter the smooth curve on the right edge (Fig. 9-3B).

For the right side, tilt the brush tip to the left and exert pressure while letting the tip travel along the left side. Lift the pressure and straighten the brush handle, then extend the tip (Fig. 9-3C).

Fig. 9-3 Leaf

A. Leaf Facing the Right   B. Left Side Stroke   C. Right Side Stroke

Leaves Facing the Left

Just reverse the above movements — a piece of cake if you are left-handed! (Fig. 9-4)

Fig. 9-4 Leaves Facing the Left

Foreshortened Leaves

When leaves are coming toward the viewer, their stems are hidden and only the tip halves show. These leaves are short and fat, with their top sides flattened and showing a groove in the middle (Fig. 9-5A). When these foreshortened leaves face right, do the left side of the leaf as follows: Hold the brush obliquely, allowing more body to be in contact with the paper. Tip the point to the left. Make the stroke fat and short (Fig. 9-5B). For the right side of the leaf, begin a distance away from the start of the left side. Develop a valley between the two shapes. Scoop downward and then lift by straightening the handle and allowing the tip to extend outward from the middle of the two shapes (Fig. 9-5C).

Fig. 9-5 Foreshortened Leaf, Facing Right

A. Full   B. Left Side   C. Right Side

Note the appearance of foreshortened leaves facing to the left (Fig. 9-6).

Fig. 9-6 Foreshortened Leaves Facing Left

Folded Leaves

When leaves fold upward, the center vein travels along the baseline, the lower shape shows the underside, and the top shape shows the topside of the leaf (Fig. 9-7).

Fig. 9-7 Folded Leaf

Leaves Facing the Right

To make the lower part of the folded leaf, hold the brush handle slightly tilted with the tip pointing toward you. Begin with no pressure and allow the brush tip to travel along the baseline. Present the baseline with a soft curve (avoiding a straight line), gradually exert a little pressure, then lift the pressure and continue to extend the tip farther. The grace of the stroke relies on the curved baseline, the extended slender root and tip, and forming a body which is not too wide (Fig. 9-8).

Fig. 9-8 Lower Portion of Folded Leaf

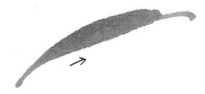

Do the top portion as follows: If the leaf is moving away from the viewer, the topside shows more on the left side of the lower shape (Fig. 9-9A). If the leaf is moving toward the viewer, the topside shows more on the right side of the lower shape (Fig. 9-9B). As you paint the top shape, move the brush in the same way as you did for the lower shape.

Fig. 9-9 Folded Leaf

A. Moving away from Viewer

B. Moving toward Viewer

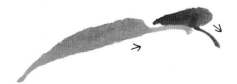

Try to present the two shapes with "valley and hills" formations; do not let them form a monotonous edge (Fig. 9-10).

Boo-boo Pad

Fig. 9-10 Monotonous Folded Leaves

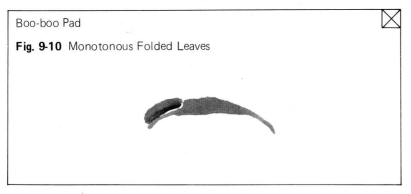

To make folded leaves going to the left and facing the right, simply reverse the process (Fig. 9-11).

Fig. 9-11 Leaves Facing Right

When the leaf is drooping or facing downward, the center vein is on top and the top edge of the shape should be a smooth curve.

To do the topside, begin the stroke with less pressure and allow the bristle tip to travel along the lower edge while exerting pressure. Lift the pressure gradually; then extend the tip along the top edge of the shape. Depending on the angle of the leaf, the underside can be shown in the front, behind the topside, or not at all (Fig. 9-12).

Fig. 9-12 Downward Folding Leaves

Turning Leaves

The turning leaf is composed of two overlapping triangles which share one side. As you see in Figure 9-13A, line A on the bottom must be aimed at point B on the top. The center vein of the two shapes in the turning leaf should connect. The topside should show a "valley" to enhance the idea of turning. An elongated edge tip serves as a bridge to smoothly carry the transition from one side of the leaf to the other (Fig. 9-13B).

Fig. 9-13 Turning Leaf

A. Triangular Shapes

B. Center Vein, Bridge, and Valley

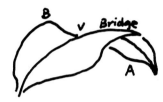

When a turning leaf faces to the right, work the first stroke on the topside with an abrupt stop to form a triangular shape. The second stroke first matches the width of the first shape and then extends along the right side to build a bridge. The second stroke can also be worked from the opposite direction if it is easier for you (Fig. 9-14).

Fig. 9-14 First and Second Strokes, Turning Leaf

Work the underside by making sure its left side aims toward the top point of the first stroke (Fig. 9-15).

Fig. 9-15 Third Stroke Aiming toward Top of First Stroke

When the turning leaf is facing the left, begin the first stroke by forming the center vein bridge, then stroke downward as with a regular leaf stroke. The second stroke begins with pressure and with the brush tip obliquely pointed to the left. Move down along the vein; then straighten the handle as you complete the stroke. Add the underside with one or two strokes (Fig. 9-16).

Fig. 9-16 Turning Leaf Pointing Leaf

Veins and Stems

The camellia has sturdy leaves with noticeable center veins. The side veins are not as impressive, and most painters elect to use only the center vein to give the "bone" to the leaves.

Although in reality the vein is light, most artists prefer to use a dark color to give more strength to the leaf. For example, they would probably use a thick dark green (dirty yellow with indigo). The vein of the topside of the leaf is done with dark green, with strong indigo and ink added. The underside is lighter, usually without the ink.

The vein is done with the Idea or Basic-Hard brush. Keep the body of the brush dry, load the bristle tip with the above-mentioned colors, and work the vein onto the leaf while the leaf is still wet. The root area is heavier and the tip is narrower. Use the movement of the arm, not the fingers, to work the vein. Maintain the vertical position of the brush at all times.

Usually the vein follows the natural division of the leaf strokes. When leaves are shown in profile, the vein lines are not painted.

After the branch is painted, a short stem is added to the root of the leaf to link the leaf onto the branch. The stem is a bone stroke done with the Idea or Basic-Hard brush. Its color can be either strong dark green or light green, depending on the colors of the leaf (Fig. 9-17).

Fig. 9-17 Leaf Studies Showing Center Veins

Branches

Key Ideas

All the branches are done with the bone stroke. The nature of the stroke is revealed by the starting pressure turn, travelling with the bristle tip at the middle of the stroke, and ending with the pressure withdrawn.

Although the branches are straightforward by nature, a slight curve can help to bring grace to the movement and formation of the painting (Fig. 9-18).

Fig. 9-18 Bone Stroke for Branches

Preparation

Use the Idea, Big Idea, Basic-Hard, or Orchid Bamboo brush. Dilute burnt sienna or vermillion into a weak puddle (about 3 teaspoons); mix a little ink to make a transparent dark brown. Dry the bristle body and load the tip 1/3 with the weak dark brown.

Method

For each section use the bone stroke as described, projecting a slight curve (Fig. 9-18). For a heavier trunk, the brush bristle can turn to a slightly oblique angle (Fig. 9-19).

Fig. 9-19 Heavy Branch Section

For a turning branch, make sure the first section completes all phases of the bone stroke. Then start the turning section inside the side edge and near the top of the first stroke. Do the turning section with another bone stroke. Continuous branching should be done with variation and grace (Fig. 9-20).

Fig. 9-20 Turning Branch

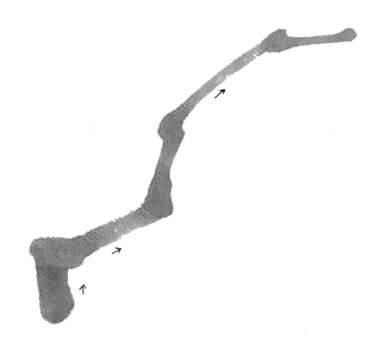

Do not turn without completing the movement of the first stroke. In nature, the turn of a branch usually occurs through branching out from the mother branch. A branch does not bend like the tool people used to start a car in the 1940s (Fig. 9-21A). Make the joint by overlapping the turning branch onto the mother branch. Do not leave a gap (Fig. 9-21B). Be sensitive about the shape at the turning area; soften the coarse ending (Fig. 9-21C) by smoothing it out with a turning stroke. Keep the turning angle less than 90 degrees (Fig. 9-21D). Vary the width of each branch according to the branching order. Do not reverse the order, and do not keep the sections the same width (Fig. 9-21E) or reduce the size of sections too drastically (Fig. 9-21F).

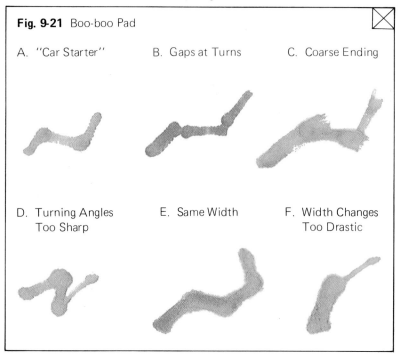

Fig. 9-21 Boo-boo Pad

A. "Car Starter"   B. Gaps at Turns   C. Coarse Ending

D. Turning Angles Too Sharp   E. Same Width   F. Width Changes Too Drastic

There are three all-time common symptoms or mistakes made in continuous branching.

The "Bamboo" Syndrome

We tend to make each section an identical length. Every three seconds, we have the impulse to pause (Fig. 9-22A). To break this habit, think long, short, medium, and extra long in a continuous movement.

The "Zig Zag" Syndrome

Why is it that every time we move left, the next move seems to go right? When we turn downward, why do we like to turn upward the next time? (Fig. 9-22B) Try to remember to turn right and then right again sometimes. Repetition is fine, but not more than two times in succession.

The "Loop-the-Loop" Syndrome

When projecting curves in our branches, we need not think of "rainbow loops" all the time (Fig. 9-22C). Think of concave, convex, and corner turns and mix them up in an irregular pattern.

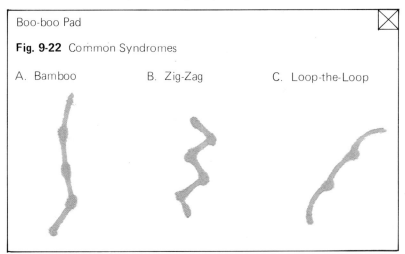

Boo-boo Pad

Fig. 9-22 Common Syndromes

A. Bamboo   B. Zig-Zag   C. Loop-the-Loop

Secondary Branching

The secondary branches are darker as they become successively smaller or narrower; add a little more ink each time you add additional branches. Tuck the roots of the secondary branches securely onto the main branch by first pressing the brush into the main branch, then moving outward (Fig. 9-23).

Fig. 9-23 Secondary Branches

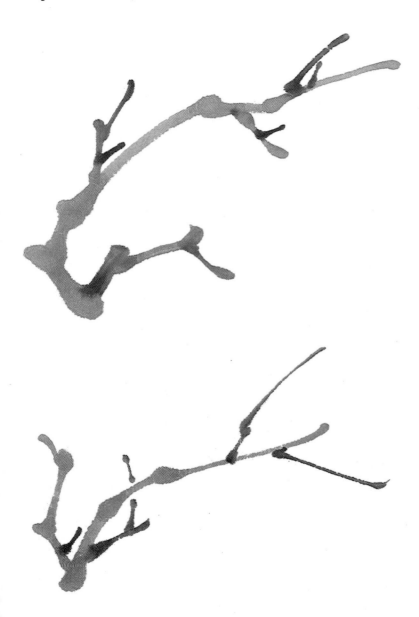

The secondary branches should grow from alternating points along the main branch. Trees in nature may have chicken feet (Ψ), but not in our paintings (Fig. 9-24A). Always join two branches first, then lead to the third branch. Avoid parallel lines in your branching (Fig. 9-24B), or branch ends which line up (Fig. 9-24C).

Boo-boo Pad

Fig. 9-24 Branching Problems

A. Chicken Foot   B. Parallel Lines   C. Ends Lined Up

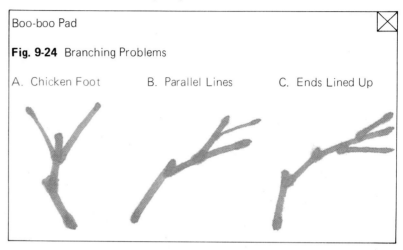

Split the angles of the secondary branches unevenly from the main branch. If they are too even, stop and change course quickly (Fig. 9-25).

Fig. 9-25 Correction of Like Angles

Branching is intended to change the angles along the main branch. Avoid having the secondary branch carry the direction of the main branch when the main branch makes a turn, as the effect of such a turn will be severely weakened by the secondary branch (Fig. 9-26).

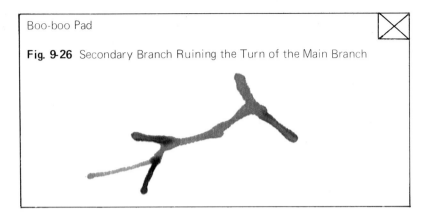

Boo-boo Pad

Fig. 9-26 Secondary Branch Ruining the Turn of the Main Branch

Branch Crossing

Branch crossing is a very important method of projecting depth, consolidating shapes, and adding interest to a composition. Crossing is done by allowing the crossing branch to show respect to the main branch; in other words, the crossing branch should be a guest to the host branch. Leave spaces on both sides of the main branch to suggest depth.

Happy Dots along the Branch

I recall quite vividly the first time I applied these dots to a branch in a classroom. There was intense curiosity among the students: "What are these!?" The thought never occurred to me that I would need to explain these dots. It is like being a southern Chinese: Our meals always have rice; likewise, in the mind of a Chinese painter, a woody branch always has dots.

What do these dots represent? They could be moss, new sprouts, a branch that never made it, things birds left behind — it really does not matter what they are. What matters is what they do.

The dots add interest to a lonely branch. They provide much-needed relief and excitement for a viewer who travels along the route of the branch. I remember as an anxiety-stricken young parent travelling with a newly potty-trained little boy in the car along Interstate 5 what a welcome sight it was to see a gas station ahead. Happy dots can be just such a welcome sight. Finally, the dots provide vital links to various elements in a composition.

To make these happy branch dots, use a dry brush and load it with the pasty ink. Dots are applied while the branches are still wet and are done with a movement similar to the start of the bone stroke. Work them at a perpendicular angle to the branch. The dot stroke can be done by pushing from the outside in onto the branch, or from the branch outward. To achieve harmony, allow the pasty ink to bleed into the branch.

The dots are grouped into clusters and displayed as host and guests. Their sizes vary according to the sizes of the branches. They should not be added excessively, or they will lose their charm (Fig. 9-27).

Fig. 9-27 Branch with Happy Dots

In our next lesson, we will study the overall composition of the camellia flower, leaf, and branch.

Lesson 10
Camellia, Part 3:
Composition

Introduction

The single-layered camellia is an ideal subject for beginning floral studies. The flowers are showy and large, fully capable of serving as the focus of attention. The clear display of each element allows us to learn the relationship between the petals, pistil, stamens, and calyx. The branches are sturdy but not monotonous and develop the flow of movement in the composition. The leaves serve as a support to the flower and develop guest clusters which balance the composition. In short, many considerations in camellia composition can be applied to many other floral subjects.

Preparation

Use the following sets of brushes or their equivalents:

The Artists' Set	The Students' Set	The Best
Flower and Bird Idea	Basic Comb. Basic Hard	Large Flow Big Idea, Orchid Bamboo

Use an 18" x 27" sheet of Double Shuen rice paper.

Prepare vermillion, red, white, and clean yellow for the flower exercise.

Pre-mix light green and dark green and prepare indigo and ink for leaves.

Dilute burnt sienna and pre-mix a little ink with the diluted burnt sienna to prepare a transparent dark brown for the branches.

Prepare some thick dark ink for veins and dots.

Step-by-step Instruction

Composition of Branches and Leaves

Before beginning your final composition, practice composing the branches and leaves. A successful composition requires that the leaves go around and have a close relationship to the branch. Without the branch, leaves have nowhere to begin. However, the leaves in front of the branch should be drawn before the branch. If the branch were drawn first, the rice paper would invariably show the branch through the leaves, even if you tried to use strong-colored leaves to go on top of the branch (Fig. 10-1). This is one of the reasons why rice paper is called the most "honest" paper.

Boo-boo Pad

Fig. 10-1 "Branch-Gate"

To confront this problem, I suggest that you use a fingernail to draw traces on the rice paper to indicate the course of the branches. These traces of branches are important to determine the location of the leaves which will reach in front of the branches, as these leaves must be done before the branch. After the front-reaching leaves are painted along the trace line, you can then paint the branches in color, threading through the leaves (Fig. 10-2).

Next you can add the leaves along the sides of the branches and, finally, the leaves which reach to the back of the branch (Fig. 10-3).

Fig. 10-2 Front Leaves Added, Then Draw the Branch following the Trace

Fig. 10-3 Additional Leaves Reaching to Side and Back

Ideally, the leaves will come out from the branch at alternating points and in directions favoring the branch movement (Fig. 10-4).

Fig. 10-4 Leaves Favoring Branch Movement

Artistically, the tips of the leaves are envisioned as radiating from the center area of the branch. The leaves on the lower portion of the branch should droop slightly downward, the middle leaves should reach sideways, and the top leaves should rise slightly upward (Fig. 10-5).

Fig. 10-5 Leaves in Radiating Pattern

In order to develop more noticeable shapes, leaves should be formed in clusters rather than scattered along the branch. The leaf cluster composition normally consists of at least two clusters reaching both sides of the branch, or three or more circling around the branches. Be aware of the angle of each leaf in relation to a circular or an oval shape. The tip area of the leaf should be formed in accordance with the circle (Fig. 10-6).

Fig. 10-6 Leaf Clusters and the Circle Formation

Occasionally, single leaves are used to support a cluster. These leaves provide balance (Fig. 10-7A), add perimeter interest (Fig. 10-7B), or serve as a liaison between shapes (Fig. 10-7C).

Fig. 10-7 Functions of a Single Leaf

Masterpiece

Now, let us begin the saga of the completion of a masterpiece.

Flowers

Flower Petals

Work a host flower, slightly off center and to the left of the paper, with space left on top. Arrange the U-shape formed by the lower petals to tilt the flower direction toward about 1 o'clock (It is never a good idea to let the flower face "high noon"). Work a bud to the left and below the host flower; arrange its angle so that it points to about 10 o'clock. This way, the root of the bud can join the main branch with the host flower like Fishes Looking for the Same Food, and together they will form a new host cluster. Place a third flower in profile at the right side of the paper, slightly lower than the bud. The profile flower serves as the guest to highlight the outstreching tendency of the supporting branch.

Calyx

Develop the calyx for each flower, locating the center base by studying the oval shape at the perimeter of the petals. Sometimes the center may not coincide with the "U." Be careful not to make the calyx too big.

Pistils

As you draw the pistils, allow their roots to point to the center and perpendicular to the calyx. Curve their tips slightly to enhance the direction of the flowers. Add a dot at the tip of each of the pistils.

Stamens and Pollen

Develop the stamens in a barrel shape surrounding the pistil. Direct their roots straight down into the calyx. (Timing is important; the petals should still be wet, but not too wet.) Then add the pollen dots.

Leaves and Branches

Branch Tracings

Use your fingernail to draw an estimated course for the branches. Draw the branch trace for the main flower perpendicular to the center of the calyx. Lead the bud in with a secondary branch. Then spring out from near the root of the main branch with another branch which leads to the profile flower (Fig. 10-8).

Fig. 10-8 Branch Tracings

Front Leaves

Before painting the branches, paint the leaves in front of the branches. Overlap a portion of the shapes onto the branch trace. (Consider these leaves as service stations on the highway.) Make sure the center veins

of the leaves can turn into the branch. Establish the center leaves of each of the clusters. Picture one supporting leaf cluster under each flower grouping, one host leaf cluster in the middle of the main branch, and a guest leaf cluster below the host leaf cluster and near the root of the main branch. These leaves are foreshortened and should be arranged with varying angles (Fig. 10-9).

Main Branches

Thread the branches through these front leaves at the designated overlapping points. Make sure you do not miss the stations, and use a few turns to develop interesting variations to the flow of the branch. Be sure the branches tuck securely into and at a perpendicular angle to the bases of the flowers (Fig. 10-9).

Companion Leaves in the Front

Establish an initial balance between the leaf groups by adding one or two leaves to each existing leaf (Fig. 10-9).

Adding Leaves to the Sides

Develop leaves reaching to the left and right sides of the branches, balancing each leaf cluster along the branches (Fig. 10-10).

Adding Leaves to the Back

To complete each cluster, add leaves reaching to the back. Allow these back leaves to overlap with the front leaves or branches to show depth (Fig. 10-10).

The Finale

Finally, add pasty ink dots and additional twigs or leaves along the branches to break monotony, add interest and variety, and help to link various clusters of shapes (Fig. 10-10).

Fig. 10-9 Leaves in Front of Branches

Fig. 10-10 Completed Camellia Composition

Fig. 10-11 Camellia

Paper: Colored Shuen (brown) rice paper.
Brushes: **Large Flow** (flower, leaf), Idea (stamens, pistil, pollen, vein),
Orchid Bamboo (branch).
Colors: vermillion, red, crimson lake, purple madder (flower); poster
white (stamens, pistil, vein), with yellow (pollen); green mixed by blending
yellow and indigo, crimson lake (calyx); green, indigo, ink (leaf); burnt
sienna, ink (branch).

柱	頂	紅
Chu	Ding	Hong
(Post)	(Top)	(Red)

Fig. 11-1

The Idea of Amaryllis

The amaryllis reflects, in a simple and yet dramatic way, the spirit of all the trumpet-shaped flowers. It is an excellent subject for showing the blend of various colors, the formation of a trumpet-shaped flower, and the method of oblique strokes.

In this lesson, the focus will be the spirit of the flower: its unique features, its formation, and its idea.

There are many types of amaryllis, each with its own name. One of the types has a pink flower. When the flower blooms, there is no leaf to cover her body. Since the flower is shy, she turns pink; therefore, she is called the "Naked Lady." I like this name a lot.

The scarlet-red amaryllis is called "Chu Ding Hong," meaning "post top red." This flower carries doubly cheerful messages: "Climbing to the top of the post" is a great omen for success; red is the color of happiness, a bountiful land, warm-hearted people, fertility, and prosperity. The flower offers the good wishes of climbing to the highest ladder of success and blossoming into multitudes of red. For people who graduate from school or get a new job, for people who first start doing brush painting, for a teacher who is offering his first televised course, the amaryllis is a "must" subject.

Lesson 11
Amaryllis, Part 1:
Flowers

The Anatomy of the Amaryllis

As stated earlier, the amaryllis is a trumpet-shaped flower. The type of amaryllis used for this study has vivid scarlet petals with a green base. The flower is huge, perhaps four or five inches across.

Petals. The petals form two sets of triangles. There are three inside and three outside petals, for a total of six. All have impressive, striped veins.

Center. The center refers to the root area of the petals. Each petal turns green near its root.

Stamens. The flower has six stamens, each with an impressive pollen dot at the tip.

Pistil. The single pistil is extra long, with three happy dots at its tip.

Trumpet. This elongated base of the flower is only seen when the flower is in profile.

Stem. The green stem receives all the petals into a knot, then extends and turns into the sheath, which joins the stalk.

Stalk. The thick, flowering stalk stands up to two feet tall, and each stalk carries up to four or five flowers. The flowers are all rooted at the top of the stalk, initially protected by the sheath.

Leaf. The leaf is broad and shaped like a strap. It sheaths the stalk on both sides (Fig. 11-2).

Fig. 11-2 Elements of Amaryllis

Materials and Preparation

Double Shuen rice paper: 13½" x 27", vertical. The longer the paper, the more elegant the height of the flower.

Use the following sets of brushes or their equivalents:

Element	Artists' Set	Students' Set	The Best
Flower Detail Leaf	Flower and Bird Idea Large Soft	Basic-Comb. Basic-Hard Basic-Soft	Large Flow, Super Flow Flow, Big Idea Lan

On the television program, the brushes used for demonstrations are: Super Flow (Extra Large Flow) for petals; Flow for details such as stamens, pollen, pistil; and Lan for leaves (which is referred to as the "King Tut" brush).

Colors: vermillion, red, yellow (clean and dirty), indigo, and poster white.

For a large, full-colored example of the amaryllis, see Plate 2, the resource book, *An Album of Chinese Brush Painting: Eighty Paintings and Ideas*, by Ning Yeh.

Brush, Moisture, and Color Chart

Element	Brush	Moisture	Colors
Petals	Flower/Bird		
Inside Ring		wet tip 1/3	medium vermillion 1/3 + strong red 1/4
Outside Ring		wet tip 1/3	medium vermillion 1/3 + medium red 1/4
Center	Flower/Bird	dry	thick light green (dirty yellow + indigo) at the tip 1/6, then use strong mix of red and vermillion to tint the body area below the tip

Brush, Moisture, and Color Chart (Continued)

Element	Brush	Moisture	Colors
Vein	Idea	dry	pre-mix strong vermillion and red at the tip 1/4, work the veins in while the petals are still wet
Stamens	Idea	wet tip 1/4	wet creamy thick white
Pistil			add a little red
Pollen	Idea	wet tip 1/4	dirty yellow + thick creamy white
Pistil Dots	Idea	wet tip 1/4	thick white
Trumpet	Flower/Bird	wet tip 1/6	colors left over from painting the outside petals (medium red + vermillion), rinse clear and dry the tip, load tip with light green
Stem	Idea	wet tip 1/4	strong light green
Seath	Flower/Bird	wet tip 1/4	diluted vermillion + weak indigo
Sheath Vein	Idea	dry	medium vermillion + indigo
Stalk	Flower/Bird	wet tip 1/3	strong light green
Leaf underside	Large Soft	wet tip 1/3	light green + strong green (dirty yellow + indigo)
topside			underside colors + strong indigo

Step-by-step Instruction

Flower

Key Ideas

The Trumpet

The trumpet of the amaryllis is directed downward. The top petals turn inward and their lower half is hidden. The folding edge forms a U-shape, and the rest of the petals come into this "U".

The "U" always appears along the same side as the trumpet tube and runs perpendicular to the tube (Fig. 11-3).

Fig. 11-3 Trumpet

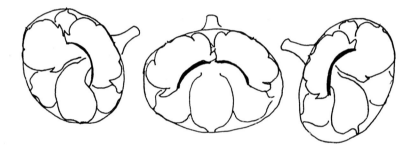

Petals are grouped into two sets of triangles with a smaller, stronger-colored, upside-down triangle on the inside, and a larger, slightly lighter triangle on the outside (Fig. 11-4).

Fig. 11-4 The Two Triangles

The inside triangle has two identically shaped petals on top. They each have two small pointed wings on their shoulders. These petals show only their top portion, with their baseline forming the U-curve. I call them the "Hats of the Flying Nun" (Fig. 11-5).

Fig. 11-5 Top Petals of Inside Triangle

Under the pair of hats, a third petal comes out like a tongue. It is thinner than the top two petals (Fig. 11-6).

Fig. 11-6 Tongue Petal in Inside Triangle

The outside triangle is formed by three similarly shaped petals. Because of foreshortening, the top petal appears smaller than the lower two (Fig. 11-7).

Fig. 11-7 The Outside Triangle

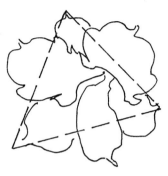

The perimeter of the flower follows the movement of a circle (Fig. 11-8A).

Allow the hat petal to form the U-shape. All of the rest of the petals curve and go through the middle of the "U" to develop the trumpet spirit (Fig. 11-8B).

Fig. 11-8 Petal Formation

A. Circular Perimeter   B. Petals Curving into a "U"

Preparation

Pre-mix a strong, light green (indigo + dirty yellow). Save this light green for filling the center.

Add about 4 or 5 drops of water to the vermillion, and about 2 drops to the red. Soften a portion of the vermillion into a medium consistency and keep the red very strong.

Loading the Brush

Using the Flower and Bird brush, dip the tip 1/3 into water and stroke off the excess moisture.

Load with medium vermillion 1/3, blend the tip on the saucer, and soften the vermillion into 1/2 the length of the bristle.

Load the tip 1/4 with some stronger vermillion. Blend slightly with just the tip portion on the saucer.

Load the tip 1/4 with strong red. Blend and soften the red into 1/3 the length of the bristle. Load the tip with strong red, then blend. Each time load a stronger color at a shorter length.

Fig. 11-9 Sample Amaryllis Flower

The Petals

The Inside Triangle Petals

To do the first Hat-of-the-Flying-Nun petal, hold the brush at an oblique angle with the tip pointing to the left. For the first stroke, land the tip, then arch up to the left to develop the "football player's shoulder." The stroke is done with 1/3 the length of the bristle in contact with the paper. The tip travels on the left side of the shape. Maintain the same position of the brush handle as you do the second, third, and fourth strokes (Fig. 11-10A).

The second stroke pairs with the first stroke to look like parentheses () (Fig. 11-10B). After completing these two strokes, move to the left and right to complete the shorter third and fourth strokes. Overlap the strokes and end the third and fourth strokes slightly lower to develop the U-curve along the baseline (Fig. 11-10C).

Add the wing dots (strokes five and six) with a scooping push to the left and to the right (Fig. 11-10D).

Fig. 11-10 Hat Petal

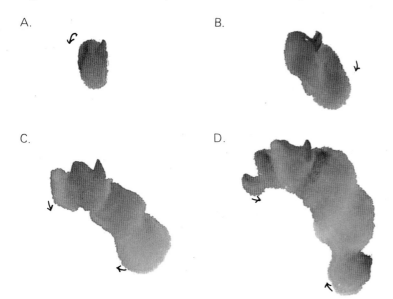

A.

B.

C.

D.

Try to follow the perimeter of the circle (Fig. 11-11).

Fig. 11-11 Flying Nun along the Perimeter of Circle

The shape of the second flying-nun petal is identical to the first, but at a different angle. Do the first stroke of this petal by showing the tip, then move upward to develop the football player's shoulder. Continue with a slight S-movement and move the stroke into the center (Fig. 11-12).

Fig. 11-12 Beginning of Second Petal

Add a short middle stroke to smooth the lower edge, then a third stroke to arch the left shoulder. As the third stroke moves into the center, leave a gap between it and the first stroke. The gap will later be filled with green to show the center of the flower (Fig. 11-13).

Fig. 11-13 Continuing Second Petal

Add two more, slightly shorter strokes on both sides if needed. Then add two dots (Fig. 11-14).

Fig. 11-14 Completed Second Petal

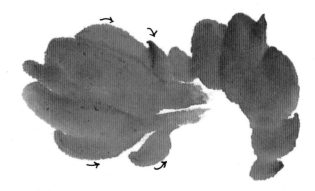

Make sure the petal stays within the upper half of the U-shape (Fig. 11-15A). Again, the petal perimeter follows the movement of a circle (Fig. 11-15B).

Fig. 11-15 Formation of Second Petal

A. Stays in Half of "U"   B. Petal along Circle

The third petal has a narrower shape than the first two, with no points on the sides. The strokes move outward from the center. Make the beginning of the first stroke perpendicular to the U, then arch to the left to widen the shoulder area. Come down with pressure (Fig. 11-16A). Use a shorter stroke to fill the middle. Leave a gap for the center green and work the third stroke like the first, but in the opposite direction. Bring the tip outward into a curve at the end of the stroke and make the perimeter follow the circle (Fig. 11-16B).

Fig. 11-16 Tongue

A. First Stroke

The Outside Triangle Petals

The outside triangle has three petals, each with two strokes worked from the outside in. The first stroke develops the tip and is worked at an oblique angle to one side. The second stroke starts inside the first and is worked obliquely to the other side (Fig. 11-17A). Curve the strokes a little so that the petal root will head toward the "U" (Fig. 11-17B). Leave a gap at the center of each petal for adding green later.

Fig. 11-17 Outside Triangle

A. Petals

B. Completion

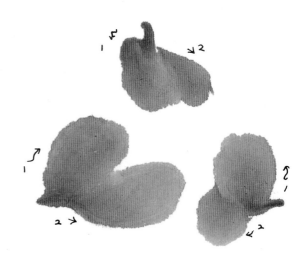

B. Outside Triangle Completion

Center Area

At the root of each amaryllis petal along the center vein the color turns green. To successfully blend the green into the existing red petals is an intriguing process.

There are two ways to prepare the brush:

After drawing the petals, the Flower and Bird brush will still have vermillion and red on it. Rinse the tip 1/6 its length in the water to clean the tip's red color. Dry the brush to control the moisture. Then dip the tip 1/6 its length into strong light green. This method of loading is more spontaneous than the alternative method, but it is harder to control the moisture. The red residue also tends to turn the green a muddy color.

For a foolproof method, use the Idea brush, wet the bristle, then dry its body. Load the tip 1/6 length with strong light green. Use another brush (Flower and Bird, for instance) to apply the strong vermillion and red on the bristle body, leaving the light green tip area alone. Encircle the light green with the red (much like Indians circling around a wagon). Blend the tip area a little. Test the colors with a stroke, pressing down to check the transition of colors (Fig. 11-18A). Do not apply the green by just travelling with the tip, since without pressing down, the green cannot blend with the red (Fig. 11-18B).

108

If you have trouble with the foolproof method, go back to the first method (I have trouble with most of the foolproof things).

Fig. 11-18 Center Area Blending

A. Green Blending into Red

Boo-boo Pad
B. Only Showing Tip Green

Apply the strokes from the edge of the "U" outward into the two inside petals. Apply them the same way at the center root of the outside petals. Make sure pressure is exerted to bend the bristle tip beyond the light green area and to allow the red on the bristle body to blend with the red on the petal. This method blends two contrasting colors harmoniously into one shape (Fig. 11-19).

Fig. 11-19 Center Green Blended

Veins

Use the Idea brush and load the tip 1/4 with a thick combination of vermillion and red. Work all the strokes from the outside edge of the petals inward with a curve. Begin the line with pressure, then lift the pressure as the line moves in. Arrange the grouping of veins into a host and guest relationship, varying interval, size, and length (Fig. 11-20A).

It is a good idea to think of the pattern of the veins as two fountains. One vein fountain erupts from the "U" and radiates to cover the first petal. The other encompasses the rest of the petals (Fig. 11-20B).

Fig. 11-20 Veins

A. Strokes

B. Vein Fountains

Fig. 11-21 Pistil and Stamens

Pistil and Stamens

Using the Idea brush, wet the tip, and load creamy white.

Pistil

Because of her length and weight, the pistil usually shows herself at the lower half of the "U". Her root comes out at a perpendicular angle to the "U" to suggest being rooted deeply into the trumpet tube. After drawing the root, bend the movement downward a little, then raise up near the tip. Maintain a similar width throughout the stroke, gradually thinning at the tip. Three happy dots sit on the tip of the pistil (Fig. 11-21).

Stamens

In grouping the stamens, try to vary the length, usually by making shorter stamens on the sides. Make the tips end unevenly so that the pollen dots do not form a noticeable line. After all, the stamens are fighting for the attention of the pistil . . . Don't we want to have a winner to ease her worries? Embrace the pistil with these stamens. Add strong yellow with white, and work a vertical dot at the tip of each stamen as the pollen dot. The pollen is big and impressive (Fig. 11-21).

While crossing among these stamens is a very good idea, it is usually preferable to have one crossing another, or one crossing two. It is not a good idea to have two crossing two (tic-tac-toe) (Fig. 11-22A) or one crossing three (fence) (Fig. 11-22B).

Be aware that all these lines are heading toward the root of the trumpet tube and do not join their roots at the edge of the "U" (Fig. 11-22C). They may turn at the tip, but try not to bend their roots too much (Fig. 11-22D). Keep the lower portions straight so the lines head straight into the root of the trumpet.

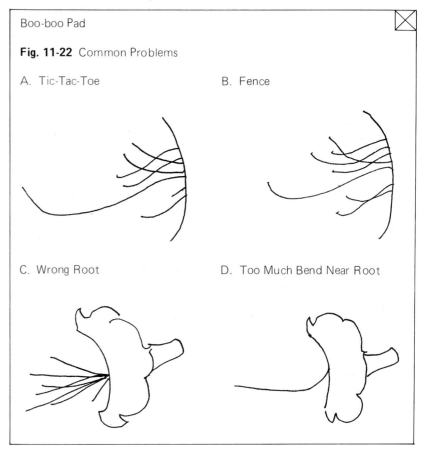

Boo-boo Pad

Fig. 11-22 Common Problems

A. Tic-Tac-Toe

B. Fence

C. Wrong Root

D. Too Much Bend Near Root

The elements which join and support the amaryllis flower will be discussed in the next lesson.

Lesson 12
Amaryllis, Part 2:
Composition

Introduction

In the last lesson, you learned the "star" of the amaryllis show. It is time to furnish the star with all the important supporting cast.

Step-by-step Instruction

Trumpet Tube

Use the Flower and Bird brush for the trumpet tube. The colors are similar to those used for the center area. Use vermillion and red on the bristle body and strong light green at the tip. Only the tip has a little moisture; keep the bristle body dry.

Work the two sides of the trumpet and use a smaller stroke in the middle. The strokes can work from either direction. Show the strokes by leaving a slight gap between them. This will help to add interest and sturdiness to the trumpet. Load the mixture of medium vermillion and red at the tip of an Idea brush and add a few veins while the trumpet is still wet (Fig. 12-1). Do not make the trumpet appear to be solid or wet.

Fig. 12-1 Trumpet Tube Strokes

Develop the trumpet root with some width to the stroke. Do not make the strokes come to a point (Fig 12-2A), as the trumpet needs to be secured onto the stem. Make sure the opening of the trumpet does not curve too widely (Fig. 12-2B).

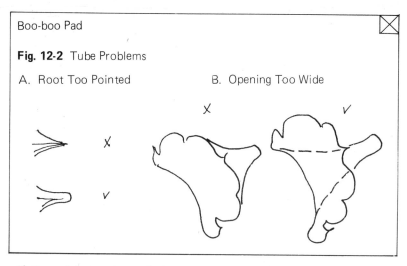

Boo-boo Pad

Fig. 12-2 Tube Problems

A. Root Too Pointed   B. Opening Too Wide

If the petals are shown facing the viewer, the trumpet tube will not be shown. If the flower is at an angle, the trumpet will be shown, but be careful not to overextend its length (Fig. 12-3).

Fig. 12-3 Side and Front Views of Amaryllis

Stem

Use the Idea brush and load the tip 1/4 length with strong light green.

Working a bone stroke, join the stem to the root of the trumpet. Follow the direction of the trumpet for the first section of the stem, then turn downard to develop the second section. Lift the stroke up near the root (Fig. 12-4). Make the turn graceful, and not too abrupt.

Sheath

Use the Flower and Bird brush and load diluted vermillion with a little indigo and ink. Work the first stroke downward, with the edge of the stroke in contact with the root of the stem. The second stroke can move either down or up, wrapping around the first stroke. The base of the sheath should be wide so that it easily joins the wide stalk.

For the vein on the sheath, load a medium-toned mixture of indigo and vermillion at the tip of a dry Idea brush. Work a few veins along both sides of the sheath near the lower area while the shape is still wet (Fig. 12-4).

Fig. 12-4 Stem and Sheath

Flower Reachinbg to the Brack

Use the Idea brush and load strong light green for the stem. Work a stroke which begins pointed, moves with increasing pressure, then turns downward into the sheath. Add two strokes on both sides of the stem with the same light green color (Fig. 12-5). Make sure to alternate the roots of these strokes slightly to avoid the chicken foot.

To work the flower, use the Flower and Bird brush. Load medium vermillion 1/3 length and medium red 1/4 length. Work two strokes to wrap the center green stroke. Work these strokes from outside in and gradually taper off the pressure (Fig. 12-5).

Fig. 12-5 First Petal on Back-Reaching Flower

Add one stroke on each side of the other two green strokes. Add additional petals to show the inside triangle. Avoid using identical heights or intervals for these petals. Try to show valleys and hills.

Using the Idea brush, add veins with the stronger vermillion and red while the petals are still wet (Fig. 12-6).

Fig. 12-6 Back-Reaching Flower

Bud

Use the Flower and Bird brush and load medium light green 1/2 length of the bristle. Rinse the tip 1/4 area and load medium vermillion and strong red at the tip. Work two embracing strokes, the first taller than the second. Develop the bud tip and move down with pressure. Pay attention to the shape on the right side. (The left side will be overlapped with a second stroke.) The second stroke starts a little lower, and the root gets more pressure than the tip.

For the veins on the bud, use the Idea brush and load the tip with strong vermillion and red. Work a few vein lines along the lower perimeter of the bud, using the idea of host and guest in the relationship between the lines (Fig. 12-7).

Fig. 12-7 Bud

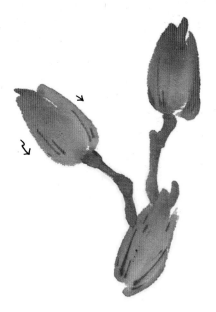

For the bud stem, again use the Idea brush, loading with strong light green. Continue the movement at a perpendicular angle to the base of the bud, draw the stem, then turn it downward into the sheath (Fig. 12-7).

Make sure the stems of the individual flowers do not form a chicken foot (Fig. 12-8A). To avoid this, lead one root behind the other, or leave a little space between the roots (Fig. 12-8B).

Fig. 12-8 Joining of the Stems

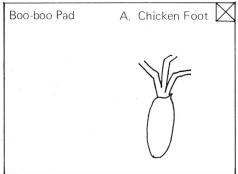

Boo-boo Pad   A. Chicken Foot ☒   B. Correct Stem Joining

Stalk

The amaryllis has a very tall, thick stalk. Although the stalk is usually erect, we prefer a slight angle in our composition.

Use the Flower and Bird brush; load strong light green 1/2 length. The brush tip should be fairly wet.

Hold the brush at an oblique angle with the tip pointing to the left. Apply enough pressure to match the root of the sheath and allow the bristle body to be in contact with the paper. However, do not have the contact much more than 1/2 the bristle length, or you will lose control of the tip. Bring the stalk down with an even pressure and lift the stroke at the very end to taper it to a point (Fig. 12-9).

If the length is not sufficient, carry the stalk off the paper, rather than ending it abruptly.

Fig. 12-9 Stalk

Leaves

Develop a puddle of green. Use the Flower and Bird brush. For the back (lighter) side of the leaf, load 1/2 length with medium light green, the tip 1/4 length with strong dark green. For the top (darker) side of the leaf, load the tip 1/6 length with strong indigo and blend the color slightly.

Key Ideas of the Leaves

The leaves sheath each other near the roots. The concept of Fishes Looking for the Same Food is again very useful.

The root area of the leaves is folded with the underside showing. In profile, the center vein travels along the lower side and the topside faces the stalk (Fig. 12-10A).

The leaves in the front of the stalk show their undersides, which are lighter (Fig. 12-10B). The leaves reaching to the back show their topsides, which are darker (Fig. 12-10C).

The leaves are wide. Most full-shaped leaves are done with two strokes. One stroke develops the tip and ends relatively higher. The other begins and ends lower to develop the root.

It is easier for right-handed artists to work the leaf stroke downward this way ↘, and upward this way ↗. But do whatever feels most comfortable.

Fig. 12-10 Leaf Strokes

Arrange the profile and the turning leaves according to the same principles discussed in the camellia lessons; however, expand the length of the leaves.

After doing the lighter underside leaves, add the profile leaves and turning leaves, as well as some leaves reaching to the back. Be aware of the distribution of the dark leaves and use them to enhance the variety in the composition (Fig. 12-11).

Fig. 12-11 Composition with Additional Leaves

If leaves overlap, make sure the back leaf leads toward and joins the root. It is important not to show the back leaf as too thin near its exposed root (Fig. 12-12A) or at too extreme an angle to reach the root (Fig. 12-12B).

Two tips can be very helpful: First, begin or end the root with relatively wider oblique strokes (Fig. 12-12C). Second, if the leaf begins with two pointed strokes, make the strokes part slightly near the root so that their outside edges can lead the viewer to the root of the plant (Fig. 12-12D).

Boo-boo Pad

Fig. 12-12 Problem Groupings

A. Back Leaf Root Too Thin   B. Leaf Not Directed To Root

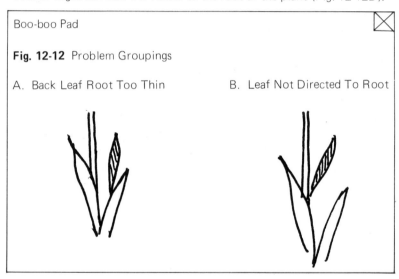

Remedies

C. Wider Root   D. Separated Stroke to Widen
                                        the Root

Leaf Composition

Fix the root point with the first leaf, not the stalk. When the end of the painted stalk is the root point, the composition is rigid, and the now much-dreaded chicken foot is almost inevitable — what horror! (Fig. 12-13)

Boo-boo Pad

Fig. 12-13 Roots All Coming to One Point

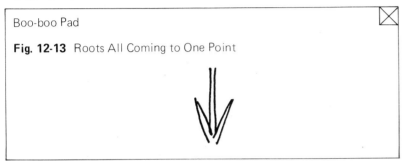

A preferred method is to lengthen the stalk with an overlapping leaf. This is more elegant and has more possibilities for variation. To overlap, visualize first the continuing course of the stalk, then lead the first leaf to establish the root (Fig. 12-14).

Fig. 12-14 A Great Way to Root the Plant

Balance the first leaf with a leaf going to the other side. Vary the angle and length of each leaf and sometimes use two leaves to balance one. Develop one side as host, the other side as guest. Determine which side needs more elements according to the need for overall balance, support for the flower, the flow of movement, and the availability and treatment of the space (Fig. 12-15).

Fig. 12-15 Amaryllis

The farther that leaves grow to the sides, the higher they should be rooted. Project an overall arrowhead at the root of the plant to show grace and depth. Do not aline the base of the leaves into a straight line (Fig. 12-16).

Fig. 12-16 Arrowhead Root

If the paper cannot accommodate the height of the plant, do not cut the plant short (Fig. 12-17A). Rather, lead the leaves off the base of the paper to a distant root point below. In this case, the baseline will become even. It is important to reveal some space among the leaf strokes to break the bucket bottom image (Fig. 12-17B).

Fig. 12-17

Boo-boo Pad

A. Plant Cut Short

B. Plant Leading off Paper

Finally, consider the total composition of the leaves and flowers, and be sure the leaf cluster is not too weak (Fig. 12-18A), and proportionally weighty enough to balance the impressive amaryllis flowers (Fig. 12-18B).

Fig. 12-18 Balance of Leaf and Flower

Boo-boo Pad

A. Leaf Too Weak

B. Proper Balance

牡 丹

Fig. 13-1

Muh
(Peony)

Dan

Lesson 13
Peony, Part 1:
Flowers

Introduction

The study of the peony serves as the "finale" to our floral studies. The following three lessons aim to provide an understanding of the different groupings, attitudes, and relationships among multiple-petaled flowers. Sensitivity to color shading is stressed to establish distinction among various components as well as to establish the depth and focus of the flower. Various criteria for composition are used in this study: host and guest, flow (tendency), and perimeter interests.

Above all, the peony lessons are intended to convince the student that complication is not the same as difficulty. If one understands basic structure, achieving satisfactory results with complicated subjects such as the peony is often easier than with simpler subjects.

The Idea of Peony

The tree peony is native to China and is called Muh Dan. The flower symbolizes good fortune and material well-being. It is the king among all flowers.

The best peony is cultivated in Loyang. The legend for this particular peony city goes back to the days of the empress Wu Zetian, the first woman sovereign in Chinese history (690-701).

One cold winter day, the empress was drinking wine in her chamber and enjoying the snowy scene outside. As she opened her window, she was greeted by the sweet smell of the winter plum blossoms. Her appetite for the fragrance of the flower aroused, she issued the following order to God:

Tomorrow I shall walk about my garden;
I bid you to make
All the flowers blossom in the night,
Before the morning wind has time to blow.

Because of her name, which means "Disciplining Heaven," and her absolute power as a ruler ordained by heaven, Zetian believed that the plants dared not disobey her. Indeed, all the plants began to bud and blossom that night, but the tree peony remained bare. Too proud to flatter the empress, it did not put forth even one leaf. In utter rage, the empress ordered all the peonies in the capital city of Xian to be banished to the town of Loyang. Once these peonies arrived at Loyang, they all blossomed with hundreds of new varieties of flowers.

The Anatomy of the Peony

Petals. Peony petals are full bodied, with shapes varying from an upside-down egg or short-handled spoon to a fan. The petals have uneven edges and deep indentations. Peonies are classified according to their layers. Each layer has five petals, and five to ten petals are considered single layered; fifteen to twenty-five are the semi-multiples. The real multiple-layered peonies can have hundreds of petals.

Seed Pod. The seed pod consists of five "female" dots which radiate out like a star and are seated above a half ball which shows at the center of the flower.

Stamens. Happy dots grouped around the seed pod form the stamens.

Calyx. Five in number, the calyx is green with a crimson tip, and short with a fully body.

Calyx Leaves. These leaves are spearheaded or spoon shaped. With an attitude of being always happy to serve the flower, they are called The Knights of Shining Armor. The Chinese also call them Swinging Belts. There are usually five calyx leaves under the root of the calyx.

Leaves. The leaves are palm shaped. There are three on each stem, with one leaf at the tip of the stem and two opposing each other near the root of the tip leaf. Each leaf may develop into three sections. However, usually the tip leaf develops the full three sections first and the two side leaves remain unsectioned. Commonly, the Chinese refer to peony leaves as Three-handled Nine Tips.

Stem. The peony stem connects the leaves to the branch; its topside is grooved.

Veins. A center vein divides each leaf in half; vein branches reach to various points on the leaf.

Branches. New branch shoots are reddish-green, sturdy, and straight. The mature branches (two years or more) are woody and rugged.

Scales. The scales, cone-shaped sprouts near the tips of branches, protect the plant through winter. They open to allow the new growth to come out.

Fig. 13-2 Anatomy of the Peony

Materials and Preparation

Paper and Brushes

Use Double Shuen rice paper.
Use the Flower and Bird or the Basic-Comb. brush for petals and leaves.
Use the Idea or the Basic-Hard brush for the seed pod, pollen, veins, calyx leaves, calyx, and branches.

In my paintings, a Large Flow brush is used in place of the Flower and Bird for the flower petals, a Large Orchid Bamboo for the leaves; a Flow (for dots and details), and a Big Idea or Orchid Bamboo is used in place of the Idea brush. These are also the brushes used in my television demonstrations.

Colors

Colors: vermillion, red, indigo, burnt sienna, dirty and clean yellow.
Poster white.
Ink.

Color Preparation

Wet the vermillion, red, and indigo with 2 to 3 drops of water; keep the colors thick.
Wet the dirty and clean yellow with 1 teaspoonful of water to soften the colors.
Add a few drops of water to the white jar; and stir the white into a creamy thick condition.
Pre-mix some vermillion with white on a saucer. The color turns into a beautiful peach. Dilute this peach mixture into a medium consistency.
Pre-mix the dirty yellow and indigo into a light green and a dark green on separate saucers; keep both greens strong.
Dilute the burnt sienna, mixing it with a little ink to turn the color into a transparent dark brown.
Mix white and clean yellow into a thick cream.
Prepare a teaspoonful of ink.

Color and Moisture Chart

Element	Brush	Moisture	Colors
Petals	Flower/Bird (Basic-Comb) (Large Flow)	medium 1/3	
front of cup			medium peach (vermillion + white) 1/3 + strong vermillion 1/6
back of cup			above colors + strong vermillion 1/4 + thick red 1/6
tutu: first layer			medium peach 1/3 + strong vermillion 1/5 + medium red 1/8
second layer			medium peach 1/3 + strong vermillion 1/6
third layer			medium peach 1/3
Bud	Flower/Bird	medium 1/3	same as the cup above
Seed Pod	Idea (Basic-Hard) (Flow)	dry 1/6	thick dirty yellow + indigo = thick light green (pre-mix)
Stamens	Idea	dry 1/6	thick white + thick yellow = thick creamy yellow (pre-mix)
Calyx (leaf)	Idea	medium 1/4	medium dirty yellow + medium indigo = medium light green (pre-mix) + strong vermillion 1/8
Flower Stem	Idea	medium 1/4	see calyx colors

Color and Moisture Chart (Continued)

Element	Brush	Moisture	Colors
Leaf topside	Flower/Bird	wet 1/3	pre-mixed medium light green 1/2 + medium indigo 1/3 = dark green, + strong indigo 1/4, sometimes + ink 1/4
under-side			pre-mixed medium light green 1/2 + medium dark green 1/4 + vermillion 1/6
young leaves			weak light green 1/3 + strong vermillion 1/6
Leaf vein	Idea	dry 1/6	thick dark green (dirty yellow and indigo) mixed with thick indigo and ink 1/3
Leaf stem	Idea	medium 1/4	a little stronger and darker than the leaf
Branch	Idea	medium 1/4	pre-mixed weak dark brown (diluted burnt sienna + ink); add pasty ink dots
Scale	Idea	dry 1/6	strong red

Alternative Colors for Peony Paintings

Peach peony: white with vermillion, vermillion, red (As shown on the television program for this lesson, these colors can be replaced by the following colors for a variety of colored peonies.)

Pink peony: white with permanent magenta, permanent magenta, crimson lake

Red peony: red with crimson lake, crimson lake, purple madder

Yellow peony: clean yellow with white, vermillion, red

For additional full-colored examples, see the resource book. *An Album of Chinese Brush Painting: Eighty Paintings and Ideas,* by Ning Yeh, Plates 9, 17, and 48.

Brush Loading

Review Lesson Eight, Camellia, Part 1, for information on loading colors on the brush.

Step-by-step Instruction

The Flower

Key Ideas

The center petals form a cup, with the seed pod at the center. The perimeter petals form an octagon shape. Follow the direction of the cup and encircle the cup in layers. I refer to the layers of the perimeter petals as the tutu. The flower is balanced on both sides. All the petals are rooted below the seed pod, like Fishes Looking for the Same Food (Fig. 13-3).

Fig. 13-3 Key Ideas of the Flower

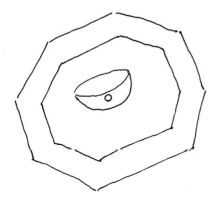

Method

Cup

Use the Flower and Bird brush for the petals and the Idea brush for the seed pod and pollen dots.

Front of the Cup

Form the bristle tip, dip the tip 1/3 into water, and stroke off the excess. Load the tip 1/3 length with the medium peach-colored mixture and reload 1/6 length with strong vermillion.

Use three strokes to form the petal in the front.

Stroke 1: Hold the brush at a 45-degree angle with the tip pointing to the left. Begin with light pressure and gradually lower the pressure while pushing upward. Allow the left side to form a ↗ curve and the right side to stay as a smooth curve ↗. Lift the pressure with a slight scooping motion (Fig. 13-4A).

All the petal strokes are based on this one. Try this stroke in various angles (Fig. 13-4B).

Fig. 13-4 Stroke 1

A. Front of Cup

B. Various Angles

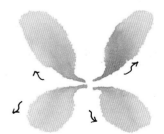

Stroke 2: This stroke is smaller, rooted higher, and overlaps with the first stroke (Fig. 13-5A).

Stroke 3: This stroke is short and fat and it starts with heavy pressure. Keep your eye on the left side. Exert pressure downward rather than allowing the stroke to travel too far. Scoop the brush clockwise to overlap the first stroke (Fig. 13-5B).

Fig. 13-5 Front Petal

A. Strokes 1, 2   B. Strokes 1, 2, 3

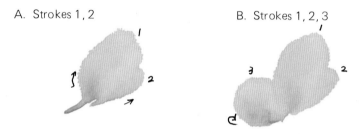

Side of the Cup

Do two to three strokes for each petal. Do the middle stroke first, elongating its shape. If the front petal is skinny, start the side petals lower. If not, start on the shoulder of the front petal. Try to present a U-curve when both sides are completed. (A little above the middle of this U-curve is the center of the flower. Make sure the rest of the strokes come from that center.) The second, inside stroke starts with a fatter root, so the shape suggests that the petal continues into the center. Add a third stroke on the outside if it is needed to break the monotony of the U-shape. The side petals should be taller than the front petal (Fig. 13-6).

Fig. 13-6 Side of Cup

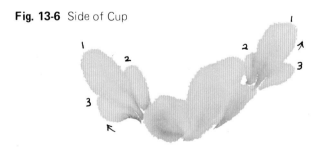

Seed Pod

Using the Idea brush, form a fine tip and load 1/6 length with thick light green. The seed pod may be hidden or partially shown, depending on the height of the front petal. Paint the top star dots first, then the little pumpkin shape below (Fig. 13-7).

Fig. 13-7 Seed Pod

Back of the Cup

Continue with the Flower and Bird brush and keep the peach color used to do the front petals on the body. Rinse the tip, stroke off the excess moisture, then load the tip 1/5 with strong vermillion and the very tip 1/8 with thick red.

The back of the cup is made up of two petals which curve toward each other. These petals are taller than the front petals, and each is done with three to five strokes.

Begin the first stroke with a fatter root by pressing the brush tip. If the shape is still skinny near the base, work two short strokes as fillers to widen the base (the shaded strokes). This will help strokes 2 and 3 point in the right direction. Avoid covering the seed pod. Seal the middle gap between the two petals with additional strokes (Fig. 13-8A).

Add two groups of strokes on both sides to show the perimeter petals in the back; they can be a little lighter and should be taller to form the top two points of the octagon shape (Fig. 13-8B).

Use a clear brush, wet it, and then dry off the moisture. Lightly brush over the seed pod and the top edges of the front petal while the colors are still wet to harmoniously blend the different elements.

Fig. 13-8 Top Petals

A. Back of the Cup

B. Top Points of the Octagon

First Layer of the Skirt

Like the tutu, the first layer of the skirt is foreshortened. Do the center petals fat and short and elongate the side ones.

Load the brush 1/3 length with peach color and the tip 1/4 with strong vermillion, then 1/6 medium red.

Tilt the brush 45 degrees; with the tip pointing to the left, do strokes 1, 2 and 3. Reverse the brush angle to do strokes 4, 5, and 6.

Lead the elongated strokes to two points on each side to form the four side corners of the octagon's perimeter points (Fig. 13-9).

Fig. 13-9 First Layer of the Skirt

Second Layer of the Skirt

Load 1/3 length with peach. Rest the brush tip sideways to establish the wide root of the petal. Use up to five strokes to form one petal. Do the center petals, then extend the side petals to form the octagon shape. Add a third layer if need. It is not necessary to fill the octagon shape solidly with petals; show some gaps along the skirt to allow room for imagination. I think of the famous scene in a movie where the skirt of Marilyn Monroe went flying high. I beg forgiveness from my forefathers (Fig. 13-10).

Stamens

Using the Idea brush, load a rich, creamy mixture of white and clean yellow. Group the dots in clusters of two or three, showing a host and guest relationship. Surround the seed pod with these dots.

The stamen dots should be full shaped. Land the dots with a scooping pressure, as if making a comma, but at the same time lift upward so the tail of the comma is not shown (Fig. 13-10).

The king among flowers has arrived. I shall share with you the various elements which fill the king's court with excitement in our next lesson.

Fig. 13-10 Second and Third Layer of the Skirt

Lesson 14
Peony, Part 2:
Other Elements

Introduction

In a way, the bud is the best choice to open this chapter. The bud is nature's most precious gift. When I look at my children, how beautiful they are at the ages of sixteen and ten, they have all the best traits my wife and I have without the withering conditions and bad habits (speaking for myself, of course). We love our children partially for that "improved model" feeling.

Step-by-step Instruction

Flower Bud

Calyx

I like to work the calyx first to house the flower bud. This way the petals can be tucked in the right way. The calyx is made up of five pieces, but usually only three are showing in profile. Use the Idea brush, load with medium light green, and load the very tip 1/8 length in strong vermillion. Do the middle piece of the calyx with two strokes that are fat at the base. The side pieces end higher; drop pressure, then lift the tip by scooping to the middle (Figs. 14-1A, 14-1B).

Bud

The peony bud shares the same concepts as the flower but is much simpler in shape. Use the Flower and Bird brush and the same colors and loading procedure used for the cup. Work the front center petal with two strokes, wrapping the strokes on top of the center calyx. Extend the side petals on both sides of the center petal; then work the darker petals on top. For the baby bud, the petal strokes can move downward (Fig. 14-1A), and for the teenaged bud, the petal strokes move upward (Fig. 14-1B).

Calyx Leaves

Five leaves, flamboyant in style, radiate from the base of the calyx. Use the same brush and colors as you did for the calyx, and use one or two strokes per leaf (Figs. 14-1A, 14-1B).

Stem and Scale

The stem is also done in the same color used for the calyx. Use the bone stroke, making it perpendicular to the base of the flower. The scale wraps around the base of the stem and links the stem with the woody mature branches. Use the Idea brush, load with strong vermillion and/or red, and scoop 2 dots near the root of the stem. The dots should be different from one another in size (Fig. 14-1B).

Fig. 14-1 Bud

A. Baby Bud

B. Teenaged Bud

Leaves

Key Ideas

Typically, one leaf consists of three sections with the center section more prominent. The two smaller side sections stay a little behind the center section.

Each section is made up of two strokes. The inside edge of each stroke should be a smooth curve to show the center vein.

The leaf stem follows the direction of the center vein of the center section (which serves as the center vein for the whole leaf). Usually, the stem of the leaf turns downward to join the branch. It is important to project a curve to the center vein to insure a smooth turning of the stem.

Present the top of the leaf with some width, and arch the side sections upward to show a "U," thus suggesting the turning leaf (Fig. 14-2).

Fig. 14-2 Peony Leaf

Preparation

Use the Flower and Bird brush. Mix a puddle of medium light green (more dirty yellow, less indigo) and a mixture of thick dark green. Soften the indigo and vermillion chips with 2 to 3 drops of water; keep the vermillion and the indigo thick. Prepare 2 teaspoons of ink.

Loading the Brush

Topside Leaves

Dip 1/4 length of the bristle in water and stroke the excess off. Load 1/2 length with light green, the tip 1/3 thick dark green, and add 1/4 thick indigo. Blend the tip area on the saucer until the indigo turns dark green.

Underside Leaves

Dip 1/4 length in water. Load 1/2 light green, the tip 1/6 dark green, and add 1/8 vermillion. Blend the tip area on the saucer until the vermillion turns into a warm green.

Movement

Front View Leaves

Center Section

To do the left side of the center section, tilt the brush tip slightly to the left and allow the bristle tip to travel along the left side in a ⤵ curve (the top section of this reversed "S" is much shorter than the lower section). Exert pressure, than relax the pressure with a scooping motion to the right. Make sure the right side of the shape remains a smooth curve without turning.

For the right side of the center section, again tilt the tip slightly to the left and exert pressure while letting the tip travel along the left side. Lift the pressure and straighten the brush, then extend the tip. Should the tip split, turn the brush handle a little to regroup the bristle (Fig. 14-3A).

Sides

If the center section is directed to the right, the left side section should be foreshortened and fuller. Begin with the right side of this section, tilting the brush tip to the right and applying the stroke with heavy pressure. Add another stroke, also with heavier pressure, to the left of that stroke (Fig. 14-3B). The right side section is thinner (Fig. 14-3C). Overlap the sides to the center section and unite them into one leaf. Show a U-shape on top to suggest the turn of the leaf (Fig. 14-3C).

In reality, the center section of the peony leaf can have three points and the side sections will also show multiple points. I shared this observation with the master peony painter of the old school, Mr. Ho Ke-min. He told me to forget it. I still occasionally make my peony leaves with the thought of multiple points in mind (Fig. 14-3D). It is comforting to know that since each peony leaf has a varied shape, one can do no wrong.

Fig. 14-3 Leaf Sections

A. Center Section

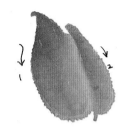

B. With left side section added

C. With right side section added

D. With multiple points

For a front view leaf reaching to the left, reverse the direction (Fig. 14-4A).

For a foreshortened front view, begin each stroke with more pressure and project a more noticeable "U" on top (Fig. 14-4B).

Back View and Young Leaves

Load the brush with medium light green 1/2 length, the tip 1/4 dark green, and add a little vermillion 1/6 length. Blend into a warm green.

For a leaf reaching to the back, do the stem first. Carry the curve of the stem with two strokes to form the center section, than add side sections (Fig. 14-4C).

The young leaves are smaller; use the same warm green color (Fig. 14-4D).

Fig. 14-4 Leaves

A. Front View Reaching Left

B. Front View Foreshortened

C. Reaching to Back

D. Young Leaves

Profile Leaves

When a leaf folds upward, the center vein travels along the baseline and the lower half shows its backside. Start strokes 1 and 2 with pressure; the shape should be wide based, fat, and short to suggest the folding. Stroke 3 follows the baseline formed by strokes 1 and 2; allow the tip to stay along the lower edge of the stroke. Exert a little pressure, regroup the tip, and extend it out. The stroke should be slender, with both sides elongated.

Since the top half of the leaf shows its topside, the colors are darker. Depending on the angle of the leaf, the top half shows either before or after its front counterparts (Fig. 14-5A).

When the leaf folds downward, the dark side is on top and the underside is light (Fig. 14-5B).

Fig. 14-5 Profile

A. Upward

B. Downward

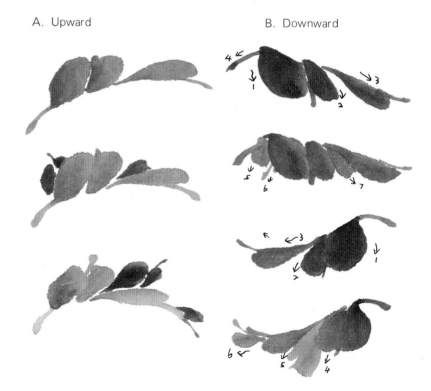

In all the profile studies, begin the strokes from the roots and start them with pressure. Otherwise, they might not show that the section is rooted onto the center vein (Fig. 14-6A).

Present the whole shape with hills and valleys by leaving some gaps between the shapes. Do not show a monotonous, flat "butcher knife" (Fig. 14-6B).

Fig. 14-6 Problem Profile Leaves

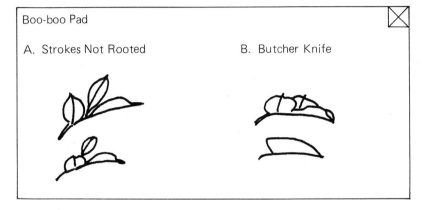

Boo-boo Pad

A. Strokes Not Rooted

B. Butcher Knife

Leaf Veins

The veins provide the bone structure to support the leaf shapes. They also enhance the direction and attitude of the leaf. Veins should be applied while the leaf is still wet to achieve a more integrated feeling.

Using the Idea brush, wet to form the tip, then stroke the moisture off completely. The body of the brush must be dry. Load 1/3 length with a mixture of dark green, indigo, and ink. Work the dark leaves first, then the light ones with a lighter color. (This could be dark green only, without indigo and ink.)

The strokes resemble fish bones. Begin with a little pressure and reduce the pressure after the initial start. Pull the brush with your arm instead of your fingers. Do not allow the tip of the brush to take off from the paper; carry the tip until the very end.

The center vein follows the joining line of the two leaf sections, and two pairs of the side veins spring out from the center vein (Fig. 14-7).

Fig. 14-7 Veins

Root the side veins securely onto the center vein. Do not detach them (Fig. 14-8A). However, sometimes the back pair can be detached from the center vein to suggest the turning of the leaf (Fig. 14-8B).

Curve the side veins inward, not outward (Fig. 14-8C). Run the veins in a vertical direction from the base to the tip of the leaf, instead of horizontally from side to side (Fig. 14-8D).

Alter the side veins and do not let them join the roots at one point (chicken foot) (Fig. 14-8E). The pattern of alternation should be consistent; if one side of the first pair begins higher, the next pair should follow the same pattern (Fig. 14-8F).

Boo-boo Pad

Fig. 14-8 Vein Problems

A. Side veins should join

B. Side veins should detach

C. Curve should go inward

D. Vertical direction preferred

E. No chicken foot

F. Alternate with consistency

132

Note that the profile leaf does not need to have a center vein drawn in. The shape already has suggested its existence (Fig. 14-9).

Fig. 14-9 Profile Leaf Veins

Branches

The new shoots of the peony branches are green or warm green; they house the leaves and the flowers. Each year they grow sturdy and smooth out of the old branches. When winter comes, the new shoots shrink and gradually turn woody. In northern China, where the weather is colder, the tree peony shrinks far more than does the peony in the south. In general, the peony in southern China grows taller than its northern brothers. Since we southerners are usually shorter than the northern Chinese, it is nice to see our southern peony can get even for us.

The mature branches are grayish-brown. Gnarled and weather beaten, like a woody rose trunk, their shapes are a dream for artistic renditions.

Use the Flower and Bird brush. Keep the body dry and wet the tip with transparent dark brown. Hold the brush vertically for thinner branches and at an oblique angle for thicker branches. Use the bone stroke. The peony branch exercises are similar to the camellia branch exercises, with a few more turning movements (Fig. 14-10).

Fig. 14-10 Branches

Add pasty ink dots to develop character and variation along the branches. Use pasty vermillion or red dots to show new growth or scale at the ends, as well as the turning corners of the branches. In comparison to the camellia branch dots, peony dots can be more pointed. Group them into host and guests (Fig. 14-11).

Fig. 14-11 Dots on the Branch

In our next lesson, we will combine all these elements into a composition.

Lesson 15
Peony, Part 3:
Composition

Introduction

This lesson reinforces some of the principles used in the camellia lessons. Emphasis is placed on developing the host flower as the focus and the guest flower and clusters of leaves as the main supportive elements. Branches are used as traveling routes to develop the flow of the painting. Depth is suggested by overlapping and crossing between elements. The various perimeter points are extended to move the viewer throughout the whole painting and to establish interesting shapes. Finally, this lesson helps the beginning artist develop sensitivity to the divisions of major spaces and to shape the spaces in and around each of the painted elements. Above all, this exercise will stress the importance of preserving the diverse virtues of all elements within a painting and of combining these elements in a spirit of balance and harmony.

Preparation

Use the Flower and Bird (Basic-Comb., or Large Flow) and Idea (Basic-Hard, or Flow) brushes and a sheet of Double Shuen rice paper (13½" x 27").

Prepare a mixture of medium peach (white and vermillion), along with strong vermillion and red, for flower petals.

Pre-mix clean yellow and white for pollen dots.

Develop mixtures of light green and dark green by using dirty yellow and indigo in varying proportions.

Prepare indigo, vermillion, and ink for leaves.

Pre-mix a little ink with diluted burnt sienna for a transparent dark brown for the branches.

Prepare some thick ink for dots.

We now commence our venture into the mysterious realm of our wonderful rice paper.

Step-by-step Instruction

Flowers

Host Flower

Work a host flower at about the middle point in relation to the height of the paper and off center to the left. Allow room below for a host and a guest cluster of leaves.

Develop the front petals of the flower center cup. Try to turn the U-shape so that the flower faces about 10 o'clock. Add the seed pod in the middle of the "U" above the front petals; then develop the back petals of the cup. Work in the first, second, and third layers of petals below and on both sides of the cup. As you add the petals, think of the octagon shape of the perimeter and the balance on both sides of the flower. It is reassuring to know that a peony flower can have up to hundreds of petals. You can keep adding them until you get the desired balance. All the petals must be done with speed to insure integration. Add the pollen dots (Fig. 15-2).

Bud

Work a flower bud above the host flower as the main guest element. Make the bud tilt slightly to the right (about 12:30). This bud will provide needed balance but still be supportive to the host flower. If the bud tilts too much or pulls too much to the right of the paper, it will rival the importance of the host.

Before starting the petals of the bud, do the calyx. Now add the front petals, then the back petals. Do the calyx leaves on both the flower and the bud (Fig. 15-2).

Leaves and Branches

Tracing Line

Use your nail to draw an estimated course for the branches. The new branches below the flower and the bud should not be turned but should be relatively straight. The older branches can show more turns (Fig. 15-1).

Fig. 15-1 Projected Branches

Fig. 15-2 Host and Bud Flowers

Fig. 15-3 Front Leaves and Branches

Fig. 15-4 Peony Masterpiece

Develop leaf clusters below the host flower. Work one dominant group on the right, one supportive group on the left. Be aware of the route of the branch and make sure the leaf stems can be led into the branch. The large group overlaps with the calyx leaves and looks somewhat like an extended layer of skirt to the flower, while the leaf on the left reaches out like a peninsula to a continent.

Work one leaf cluster below the existing leaf cluster, as a guest to the existing leaves. Overlap the center leaf with the trace of the branch and extend two leaves below the center leaf.

Develop two leaves below the bud. The host leaf should overlap the trace of the branch and the other leaf should move to the right side of the branch.

Develop the green stalk below the host flower. Aim it at a perpendicular angle to the root of the seed pod and extend it downward. Then develop the older branches with dark brown colors. Lead another green stalk below the bud, thread it through, and establish its root onto the old branches below.

Be sure to study the directions of the existing leaves to determine the proper points for the branches to cross each leaf. Follow the center vein of the leaf to locate the stem of the leaf (Fig. 15-3).

Add scale dots to join the green stalks to the old branches and ink dots to give character. Add red scale dots at the ends or the turning points of the old branches. Do all these dots while the branches are still wet (Fig. 15-3).

Develop two profile leaves, one to the left of the bud (1) and one to the right of the host flower (2), to add balance and support to the existing leaves, like islands beside the continents. Show depth by adding some darker leaves behind the branches and the existing leaves (3, 4, 5). Add a couple of leaves on the upper right of the host flower to increase the spread of its surrounding "leaf skirt" and to provide a liaison between the lower and the upper leaves (6, 7) (Fig. 15-4).

Add a guest leaf cluster crossing behind the bud stalk (1) to provide support to the existing leaves, enhance depth, and serve as a linking element between the flower and the bud. Add a green stalk reaching to the right to balance the composition. By dividing the spaces into V-shapes, the new stalk also invites the viewer to come into the painting from the right side (2) (Fig. 15-4).

Add veins to all the leaves. The masterpiece is now completed, waiting for your signature and seals (Fig. 15-4).

Here is another finished peony composition for you to study (Fig. 15-5).

Fig. 15-5 Peony Composition

Bonuses

Before we bid farewell to our floral lessons, may I offer you the following bonuses.

Fig. 15-6 Camellia

Blue Iris

Fig. 15-7 Blue Iris

Paper: Double Shuen rice paper.
Brushes: Large Flow (flower), Idea (beard), Big Orchid Bamboo (calyx, stalk), Lan (leaf).
Colors: Prussian green, French ultramarine, Winsor violet, indigo, neutral tint (flower); yellow, vermillion (beard); green mixed by blending yellow and indigo, indigo, ink (leaf).

(Use the petal stroke of the peony and the leaf stroke of the amaryllis.)

Poppy

Fig. 15-8 Poppy

Paper: Double Shuen rice paper.
Brushes: Large Flow (petal, bud), Big Idea (leaf, stem), Idea (seed pod, pollen), Best Detail (fine hair).
Colors: yellow, vermillion (petal backside); yellow, vermillion, red (petal front side); light green (seed pod); poster white with yellow (pollen); green mixed by blending yellow and indigo (leaf, hair, stem).

(Apply what you have learned in the peony lessons.)

Orchid

Fig. 15-9 Orchid

Paper: Double Shuen rice paper.
Brushes: Orchid Bamboo (leaf), Idea (petal, stamens, stem).
Colors: Green mixed by blending yellow and indigo, indigo (leaf), green with crimson lake (petal, stem), crimson lake (stamens).

Bamboo

Fig. 15-10 Bamboo

Paper: Double Shuen rice paper.
Brushes: Large Soft (trunk), Idea (ring, branch, leaf) Wash (background).
Colors: Ink (bamboo), Winsor Violer (shade) Go ahead, make your day!

Fig. 18-13 Landscape Coloring

Fig. 18-14 Completed Landscape

An exciting landscape demonstration is offered in Lesson Eighteen. Please check the list of materials in case you wish to try these paintings (Figs. 18-13, 18-14).

Fig. 16-1

Ma
(Horse)

Lesson 16
Horse, Part 1:
Head

Introduction

The physique and movement of the horse combine with rare balance the qualities of grace and strength, the harmony of the yin and the yang. To depict the spirit of the horse is to reveal the wholeness of Tao — the essence or the vitality of nature. To be successful in the exercise of the horse painting, the artist needs to capture the true meaning of the statement, "A lively painting must be executed in a lively way." Horse painting is a continuous rhythm from start to finish: no hesitation, no breakdown of movements, and no corrective effort. Ink is spontaneously blended and strokes are dynamically executed. It is one of the most dramatic presentations of the throw-ink method.

The Idea of Horse

Horse painting is my family tradition. From the very beginning, it has been a subject in which I felt I must excel. It occupies a very special place in my heart.

According to Confucius, the horse should be complimented, not for its strength, but for its virtue. In the horse, the Chinese see a spirit of rendering service without asking recognition, of suffering hardship without complaint, of offering life-and-death friendship and loyalty without seeking material gain in return, of marching humbly with the utmost inner pride. Elevated by these qualities, the horse becomes humanistic.

In Chinese folk legend, the horse is the celestial creature which blessed Chinese people with their first set of written language.

The legendary first ruler of the Chinese nation — the Yellow Emperor — prayed to heaven to give him the tools with which he could communicate with his subjects. In his dream, he saw eight celestial horses descending from heaven, each carrying a scroll inscribed with written symbols. Wherever these horses went, horse-hoof-shaped flowers (calla lilies) would blossom to celebrate their visit. Based on these symbols, the Yellow Emperor instructed his historian to construct the first written language.

In the **Book of Changes,** an authoritative Chinese classic, the strong horse signified the well-being of the Chinese nation.

The Anatomy of the Horse

The horse we are about to study is our family's creation. Its title, Celestial Horse, was given to my family by the late Prince Pu Yu, the brother of the last emperor of China. The Celestial Horse differs from the ordinary horse in several ways: its forehead is longer; its head, chest, and hooves larger; its legs, mane, and tail more elongated; and its stomach line tighter. Overall, it is a spirit that shares many of the attributes we think a beautiful human being should have, not a literal animal as judged from the scientific viewpoint of a horse breeder (Fig. 16-2).

Fig. 16-2 Horse

147

Materials and Preparation

Use the Flower and Bird, the Basic-Comb., or the Large Flow brush, Double Shuen rice paper (13½" x 27"), 5 teaspoonfuls of dark ink.

Step-by-step Instruction

Head

Line Work

Brush Preparation

After the brush tip is formed, dip the very tip into water for a little moisture, then load 1/3 length with dark ink. Stroke off the excess and regroup the tip.

The Eyes

Since the eyes will reveal the spirit and intention of your horse, they should be your starting point. The line work of the eyes is heavier to show more importance. The right eye is formed by an arch on top and two dots below.

First work the arch with a little more pressure than you will use for the rest of the lines. The arch should be slightly uneven, with the left side lower, the right side higher, the left side longer, the top and the right sides shorter (Fig. 16-3A). Work two dots in parentheses motion (), scooping the dots to make their roots join (Fig. 16-3B).

Fig. 16-3 Horse's Eye

A. Arch

B. Arch and Dots

It is important to keep the space encircled by the arch and dots open to show the light of the eye. But keep the space very small, as too big

a space could make the horse look too fearful (Fig. 16-4A). Make the eye overall a rounded shape. The Oriental horse need not have the eye of the Oriental people (Fig. 16-4B).

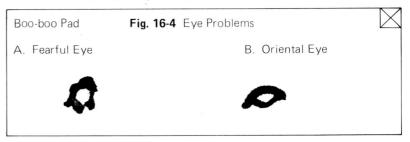

Boo-boo Pad   **Fig. 16-4** Eye Problems

A. Fearful Eye   B. Oriental Eye

To start the left eye, leave a space (a little wider than the width of the eye), and make the left eye slightly lower than the right. Start with no pressure, push the pressure to the left, then relax the pressure. Make sure the top section runs parallel to the left side of the arch of the right eye and the lower section runs parallel to the left dot of the right eye (Fig. 16-5A). If you fail to do this, your horse will look like Marty Feldman (the British comedian famed as Igor in the film **Young Frankenstein**) (Fig. 16-5B).

Fig. 16-5 Eyes

A. Parallel Relationship between Eyes

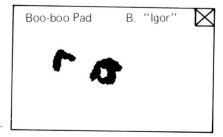

Boo-boo Pad   B. "Igor"

Right and Left Face Lines

For the face lines, follow the bottom ends of both eyes. Make the length of the left side line at least twice the distance between the two eyes. The right line can stop at the same level or a little lower than the left line. Gradually bring the two lines closer to each other (Fig. 16-6A). Be careful not to start the face lines too much inward (Fig. 16-6B) or outward (Fig. 16-6C) from the eyes. The right side should smoothly continue the movement of the left side of the eye arch (Fig. 16-6D). Do not allow the angle of the face line to deviate from the eye (Fig. 16-6E).

Fig. 16-6 Face Lines

A. Correct

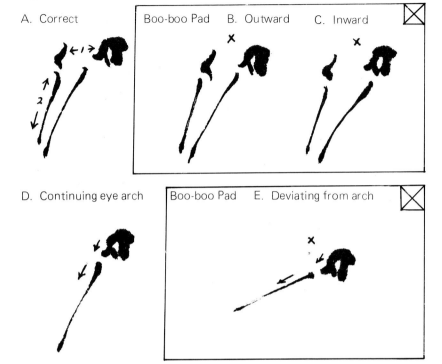

B. Outward   Boo-boo Pad   C. Inward

D. Continuing eye arch

Boo-boo Pad   E. Deviating from arch

Nostril, Upper Lip, and Lower Lip

Do the right nostril with a triangular movement, applying about the same pressure as used for the eye (Fig. 16-7A). The left side of the nostril hole softens the corner of the face. Do not try to push the corner outward or turn the corner too abruptly, causing the horse to lose all its gentle qualities (Fig. 16-7B). Make a soft turn, angle the line down below the nostril, make another soft turn, move the line up, and end the line slightly below the level of the right nostril. The right side and the lower side of the upper lip should be at about a similar distance from the nostril (Fig. 16-7C).

Start the lower lip from the curved bottom area of the upper lip. Do a small loop, then a larger one. End the lower lip below the level of the nostril (Fig. 16-7D). Do not allow a crack to develop between the two lips (Fig. 16-7E).

Fig. 16-7 Nostril and Lips

A. Nostril

Boo-boo Pad   B. Abrupt Turn

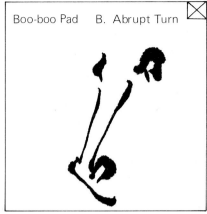

C. Upper Lip

D. Lower Lip

Boo-boo Pad   E. "Crack Up"

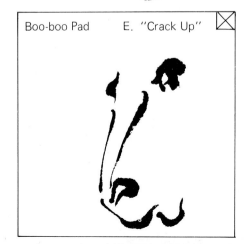

Lower Face, Cheek Lines

Start the lower face line slightly above the lower lip. Make the width between the lower and the right side face line at least twice the width allowed between the top two face lines. Move the lower line up, leaving ample space for the cheek muscle to develop (Fig. 16-8A).

The cheek line circles around the eye with a similar distance between each part of the cheek line and the eye. Sometimes the lower side of the curve is farther than the right side in relation to the eye, but we shall keep the distance the same for the purposes of this exercise (Fig. 16-8B).

Fig. 16-8 Lower Face and Cheek Line

A. Lower Face

B. Cheek

Ears and Forehead

A geometric rendering of the facial structure of the horse (Fig. 16-9A) shows that the two ears are closer than the two eyes. The distance ratio between the eye and the nostril versus the root of the ear and the eye is about two to one. Do not align the ear with the eye and nostril. For instance, the right ear should be slightly to the left of the eye-nostril line. The left ear is slightly lower than the right ear. Thread the forehead line through the ears and lead it down to the eye (Fig. 16-9B).

Fig. 16-9 Head

A. Facial Structure
B. Ears and Forehead

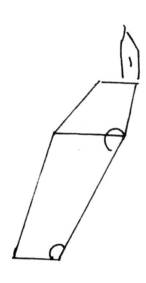 

Ink Work (Shading)

Load 1/3 of the brush bristle with dark ink. When the bristle is well saturated with ink, dip the tip in water to cause the ink to develop a slightly transparent quality. Get rid of the excess moisture.

Work the first ink shading stroke, leading its edge from the middle of the two ears to the first turn of the arch of the eye (Fig. 16-10A).

Continue from the first stroke without stopping and make the second stroke by pushing the tip along the corner of the eye (Fig. 16-10B).

The third stroke goes from left to right, still pushing around the eye (Fig. 16-10C).

By now the bristles will be bent and spread. Dip the tip in the water and straighten the hairs, but keep the bristle spread. Do the fourth and fifth strokes. Build pressure onto the face, then move down while lifting the pressure. Regroup the brush tip and shade the ears (Fig. 16-10D).

Fig. 16-10 Face Shading

A. First Stroke

B. Second Stroke

C. Third Stroke

D. Completed Head

Neck

Line Work

The Lower Line

Since in this study the head is reaching out, the lower line of the neck should come out from the top portion of the face. Make this line the same length as the distance between the eye and the lips. (I use the distance between the eye and lips as a general guide for measurements in several parts of this horse.)

The Middle Line

Do the middle line slightly above the lower line, end it a little lower than the lower line, and open the distance between the lines slightly as the stroke moves down.

The Top Line

Follow the curving arch of the forehead and make the top line short to serve as a starting point for the mane (Fig. 16-11).

Fig. 16-11 Neck Lines

Ink Work

Prepare the brush the same way as for the ink work on the head. Notice that all the ink strokes of the neck start inside the face. Begin with pressure, then relax the pressure as the stroke travels downward. Keep the brush vertical and let the tip spread when the pressure is exerted.

Do the first stroke below the top neck line. Work the second stroke on top of the middle neck line and the third stroke in between the first and the second strokes. The fourth stroke should be between the middle and the lower neck line (Fig. 16-12).

Fig. 16-12 Neck Shading

Mane

The mane is one of the most spirited elements in our horse. Use the darkest ink and stress the name by lengthening it to reveal its beauty.

To prepare the brush, load 1/3 length with a generous amount of the darkest ink, splitting the tip slightly.

Ideas

In the movement of this exercise, the mane blows in a horizontal direction as carried by the wind. Develop the mane into host and guest groupings. Use concave and convex movements to form triangular shapes, with a large triangle on top and a small one below (Fig. 16-13A). The mane does not come out perpendicular to the neck line (Fig. 16-13B).

Fig. 16-13 Mane
A. Mane Strokes

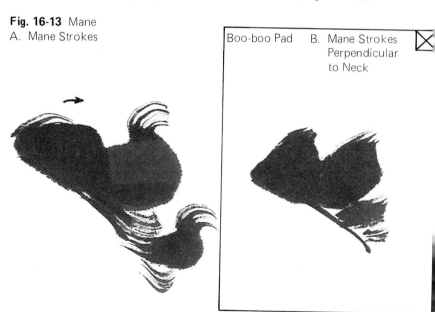

Boo-boo Pad   B. Mane Strokes Perpendicular to Neck

Using arm movement and holding the brush vertically, let the bristle tips trail the brush. All the loose mane hairs are actually traces of the bristles (Fig. 16-14A). Do not point the tip upward and use the side of the bristle (Fig. 16-14B).

Fig. 16-14 Actual Traces of Hair

A. Traces of Bristles

Boo-boo Pad   B. Mane Painted with
                Side Bristles

Strokes

In each of the mane groupings, use the following movements:

Movement 1:   Set pressure along the neck line, then spring out in a concave motion while relaxing the pressure (Fig. 16-15A).

Movement 2:   Keep the brush tip split and begin with light pressure; move the stroke out and set the pressure a little distance away from the neck line. Then spring the stroke up and relax the pressure (Fig. 16-15B).

Movement 3:   Make this stroke similar to the first movement, but smaller (Fig. 16-15C).

Fig. 16-15 Mane Movements

A. Movement 1   B. Movement 2   C. Movement 3

Add a couple of similar but smaller strokes around the ears. You now have mastered the strokes for painting the completed head of the horse (Fig. 16-16).   In our next lesson, you will learn how to paint the body of the horse.

Fig. 16-16 Completed Horse Head with Mane

153

Lesson 17
Horse, Part 2:
Body

Introduction

In our family's thinking, horse painting must be executed with continuous movement. Each stroke prepares the brush for the next stroke. If the procedure of this lesson plan is followed with constant practice, there is no need to change brushes or to test ink values. Every part of this horse is naturally integrated.

Painting the horse's body, legs, and tail continues the same principles used for the face, neck, and mane. The process is accomplished through a combination of line and ink work and careful consideration of the proportional relationships. While action is suggested by the horse's eyes and by the mane blowing in the wind, the positioning of the horse's legs and the lively movement of the tail truly bring the horse to life.

Step-by-step Instruction

Chest

Key Ideas

In this particular study, the body of the horse can be pictured as a rectangular box drawn in perspective, with the chest as its front end (Fig. 17-1). With our horse, the chest is slightly exaggerated. This follows a tradition among Chinese horse painters, who have tended to make the chest and the horse hooves larger than life. One of the reasons for this tradition is that the best horse paintings in the past were the works of the court painters, who were painting the finest breeding horses in the royal court. In the old days, the horse was as important a weapon as today's ships and planes. In order to glorify the power of the royal court, horse paintings were exaggerated to show strength.

Fig. 17-1 Box-shaped Horse Body

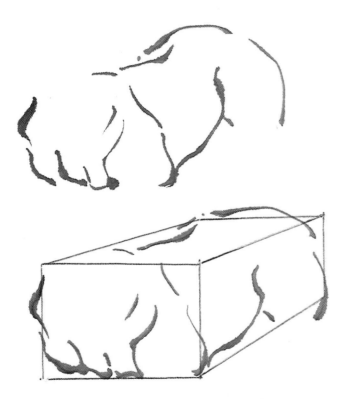

Line Work

There are five groups of lines in our chest study. The first line begins at the end of the lower neck line. Push the stroke to the left to develop the first loop, which shows the muscle, and continue to a second loop downward. Then make a corner turn to develop the edge of the box (Fig. 17-2).

The height of the chest is the same as the distance between the eye and the lips (Fig. 17-2).

The second line starts low, at the midpoint between the tip of the first loop of the first line and the middle neck line. Lead the line down, parallel to the second loop of the first chest line, and turn along the base of the imaginary box (Fig. 17-2).

The third line is the shortest, representing the center of the chest. It is directly below the middle neck line. Move the stroke down, then turn along the imaginary box (Fig. 17-2).

The fourth step in the chest lines is actually two groups of lines. Before doing these strokes, rinse the bristle tip a little to dilute the ink into a medium tone.

For the top group, make two lighter lines running parallel to the first loop of the first chest line (Fig. 17-2).

The lower group is one curving line coming downward to join the baseline and is the counterpart of the second chest line (Fig. 17-2).

The direction of the fifth line follows the top neck line and is worked opposite to the first chest line (Fig. 17-2).

The distance between the fourth and fifth line can be a little wider than the distance between the first and second line.

Fig. 17-2 Chest Lines

Fig. 17-3 Chest Ink Work

Ink Work

The ink shading on the chest is done with two wide, dark strokes from the top down on the left side. To show muscle indentations on the left side of the chest, dilute the ink at the brush tip and add a few lighter dots (Fig. 17-3).

Front Legs

Key Ideas

The structure of the front legs is pictured as having three sections. The length of the first section is the same as the second and third sections combined and is the same or a little longer than the distance between the eye and the lips (Fig. 17-4B).

Since the soul of the leg is in its third section, we like to exaggerate its length. It is this section which gives the freedom of movement in our horse.

The movement of the front legs has the range as shown (Fig. 17-4C). Be merciful — do not break the legs of our beloved horse! (Fig. 17-4D)

Line Work

The line work sequence is shown in Figure 17-4A.

Fig. 17-4 Front Legs

A. Sequence of Strokes

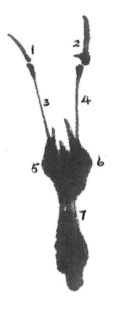

B. Proportions

C. Range of Movement

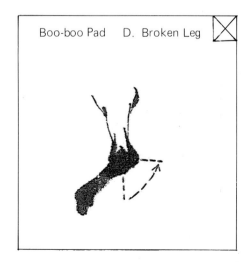

Boo-boo Pad   D. Broken Leg

Note that strokes 1, 2 and 5, 6 vary according to the angle of the legs (Fig. 17-5).

Fig. 17-5 Line Variations of the Front Leg

Stroke 7 is a variation of the bone stroke. Begin the stroke with a point, then exert pressure as you move into the stroke. Once the width matches the knee lines, relax the pressure to turn the tip of the bristle. Move the stroke down with even pressure to make the second section of the leg. Apply more pressure to make the joint. Then relax the pressure, turn the brush tip, and make the third section. Make sure the bristle tip always trails behind the brush and stays in the middle of the stroke. Also note that the beginning of the stroke points to the middle of the first section of the leg (Fig. 17-6).

Fig. 17-6 Stroke 7 of the Front Leg

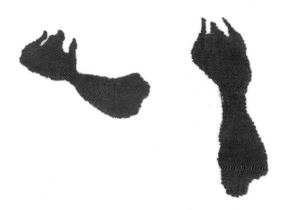

Use lighter ink for the closer leg; dark ink for the farther, or "shadow," leg (Fig. 17-7).

Ink Work

The first section of the lighter leg has no ink work, just a couple of light dots to indicate the muscle indentation. The purpose of these dots is to smoothly phase the dark, lower sections into the light, top sections. The shadow leg ink work is done with the same method as the lower strokes on the face. Load 1/3 length of the brush with ink, dipping the bristle tip into water to create some transparency; stroke off the excess moisture. Work two strokes down and two up, first using pressure on each stroke, then releasing. The above-mentioned technique is a very effective way to show the tension of muscles. Again, make sure the brush is vertical at all times (Fig. 17-7).

Fig. 17-7 Front Legs

Body

Key Ideas

Again consider the rectangular box shape of the horse's body. As you paint the horse's body, think of the body of a greyhound and the fact that we often use a belt to tighten our waistlines in order to show more spirit. Do not allow the body to become too heavy, having a sagging stomach.

Line Work

Stomach Line

Using dark ink, follow the baseline of the chest, moving the line by lifting slightly upward. The length is flexible and depends on the angle of the body. For our purposes, let's make it approximately the same as the width of the chest. At the end, make a turn upward. The upward section of the line no longer represents the stomach, it divides the stomach area and the hindquarters (Fig. 17-8).

Top Lines

Again picture the rectangular box and imagine where the top edge crosses the top of the chest. Find the middle point of this edge and extend a parallel line along the stomach. You should be able to see roughly where the back line should be (Fig. 17-8). Using lighter ink, extend the neck down if needed. Follow the neck with a concave curve for the withers and add a smoother, convex line for the back. End the back line a little shorter than the stomach line (Fig. 17-8).

Fig. 17-8 Line Work, Horse Body

Ink Work

Load 1/3 length of the bristle with dark ink and dip the tip in the water to soften the ink a little. Work a couple of strokes to define the stomach from the chest. Follow with a series of slightly curved, overlapping strokes to reflect the ribs. Be sensitive about the variations of the spaces among these strokes. Gradually make the strokes lighter as you move toward the rear of the horse. Add a few lighter dots on top (Fig. 17-9).

Fig. 17-9 Ink Work, Horse Body

Hindquarters

Key Ideas

Picture the box again. In reality, the rear of the horse is wider than the chest; but since it is farther away from us than the chest, we can picture its width to be roughly the same as the chest. A portion of the rear is hidden behind the body (Fig. 17-10).

Line Work

Using light ink, work the rump with a short line on the left (imagine that the major portion of the left side is hidden), then a short line crossing the extension of the back line; follow it with two curves downward. Extend from the turning point of the stomach line with another line, slightly closing the gap. Add a few light dots for muscle indentations. The area of the thigh is wider than the chest (Fig. 17-10).

Fig. 17-10 Hindquarters

Back Legs

Key Ideas

The back legs are structured a little differently from the front legs, and their relationship with the body is different (Fig. 17-11A).

The ratio between the sections of the leg is the same as for the front legs: The first section is the combined length of the second and the third sections (Fig. 17-11A).

The movement of the leg has the range shown in Figure 17-11B.

The back legs work in a reverse direction from the movement of human legs. Please do not turn the joint the other way (Fig. 17-11C).

Fig. 17-11 Back Leg
A. Strokes   B. Movement Range

Boo-boo Pad   C. Broken Leg

Line Work

For the closer leg, use light lines; for the shadow leg, use darker lines.

On the left side of the closer leg, move down from the body, then angle to the right and extend with another line. For the right side, use a couple of lines to soften the transition from the hip so the angle will not be too sharp and unnatural. Then extend in the direction of movement. The joint is made with the left side short, the right side more developed. Extend the back leg with a bone stroke in the same way as you did with the front legs (Fig. 17-12).

To determine where to start the farther back leg, picture the body box and the distance between the two front legs. The top section of the farther back leg is partially hidden. The first section is shorter than the rest of the legs and it tapers from wide to narrow quite drastically. The lower sections, however, should maintain the same length as the other legs. Normally, this leg should land higher. Work the ink for the back legs in the same way you did for the front legs (Fig. 17-12).

Fig. 17-12 Back Legs

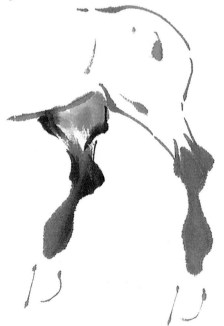

Hooves

Key Ideas

Each hoof is done immediately following the strokes of each leg, rather than waiting until all the legs are done. This will help to keep the integral continuity of the movement.

The hooves are done with the lightest ink to allow the celestial horse to "roam in the air." A gap is kept between the leg and the hoof to enhance the freedom of motion (Fig. 17-13A).

When there is an angle of movement, the leg and hoof may be foreshortened accordingly (Fig. 17-13B).

Fig. 17-13 Hoof
A. Hoof and Leg   B. Foreshortened Hoof

Line Work

Pre-mix the light ink, dry the brush, form the tip, and dip only the tip with light ink. Control the moisture.

Move the hoof lines according to the angle of the legs, as shown in Figure 17-14.

Fig. 17-14 Hoof Lines According to Leg Angle

A. Leg Reaching   B. Leg in Front View   C. Leg Reaching to the Back
   to the Front

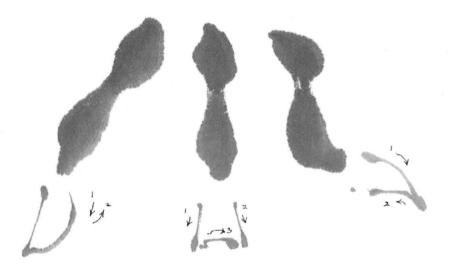

Tail

Key Ideas

Since the tail is the "finale," give all you've got for the spirit of joyful celebration.

Method

Use the darkest ink, saturate the brush well more than 1/2 the length of the bristle, and split the tip a little.

Extend the tail from the back line, estimating the starting point of the tailbone. Start the tail by moving upward at an angle; establish the pressure. Let the brush split open, carry the stroke with a couple of waving motions, then let go.

Add a few more strokes, making clusters of host above and guest below. To break monotony in the upper edge of the tail, occasionally add strokes on top (Fig. 17-15).

Fig. 17-15 Tail

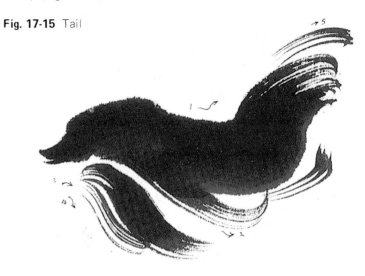

You now know the secrets of our horse painting. It is up to you to experience and express the many dynamic moods of this noble creature (Fig. 17-16).

Fig. 17-16 The Celestial Horse

Fig. 18-1   Shan   Shui
(Mountain)   (Water)

Lesson 18
Landscape
Demonstration

Introduction

Landscape painting has been the dominant school in the history of Chinese brush painting. Extensive divisions of styles, methods, and spiritual expression have been developed over the past two thousand years. Even the various elements of landscape — rock texture and formation, tree dots, cloud patterns, structure and figures — have different schools, with artists spending their lifetimes trying to perfect certain dots or texture lines.

One half-hour video instruction on landscape painting is hardly enough to scratch the surface. In this lesson, I only hope to provide some guidelines to help students appreciate the essence of a Chinese landscape painting: its tranquil theme; the contrast and harmony of land and water; key considerations in composition; samples of different approaches and emphases; and demonstration of the basic steps for doing a landscape using Chinese brush techniques.

General Discussion

Chinese landscape, termed Shan-Shui, reflects the harmonious union between the land (Shan) and the water (Shui). Land represents strength, substance, texture; it forms the major shapes of the landscape and is considered the male element. Water is frequently shown as space with some shading. Water comes in the forms of a river, lake, stream, or waterfall or as mist, cloud or snow. Water represents the spirit of grace; it is the female element. Water threads through the shapes to integrate the flow of a painting, to separate the shapes, and to highlight the forms.

When one sees spirited mountains, the description that comes to mind usually relates to majesty, grandeur, or solidity. Standing in front of a tall mountain, one senses a mood of awesome tranquility. It is like being in an open temple, silently communicating with nature.

When mountains are visited by misty clouds, however, they instantly turn soft. Their bodies are concealed in shading and their shapes are turned into silhouettes of ever-changing patches. They show some of the peaks and canyons which become lost in the grand mass of their usual shapes. Mist reduces the immediate presence of mountains to a gentle distance. It causes one to become eager to unveil the mystery of the mountain.

Chinese brush artists have been particularly attentive to the contrast and the integration of land and water in order to bring the true essence of nature into their works.

Trees and plants are the happy children of land and water. They provide a link between the two parents, break monotony, and bring depth and scale to the painting. Traces of human activities and structures serve the same purpose. The Chinese never take the view that man has the power to conquer nature. Rather, most figures and structures in the paintings are there to signify the grand scale of nature. However, houses, boats, bridges, and people can also provide points of interest and help focus the viewers' attention.

Approaches

In some of my landscape paintings, particular emphasis has been stressed on line work. The Hwa Mountain (West Hill) typifies such emphasis (see the resource book, *An Album of Chinese Brush Painting: Eighty Paintings and Ideas,* by Ning Yeh, Plate 42). The traditional approach to Chinese landscape painting was line-oriented. Founded in northern China, this school established a series of stylized line work depicting various rock formations. However, in southern China, a spontaneous blending of strokes and ink dots freed painters from the rigid formula of stylized line work and made landscape painting a much more dynamic instrument for revealing the contrast and harmony of the various elements. Recently, the Ling-nan (Cantonese) School of painters has injected more colors into landscape renditions. In most of my landscape paintings, the combined influences of the southern and Cantonese schools are quite

apparent. A wide range of versatility among other schools exists in the approaches of Chinese landscape paintings.

The approaches can vary, but rarely has it been the intention of Chinese painters to present a photo-like, realistic study of specific scenery. Chinese artists may travel, read, or collect photos or sketches of different sceneries to be used as references. But when the artist faces the paper, the playful blending of strokes, ink washes, colors, and dots takes over. The painting becomes a representation of the sphere of the artist's mentality. It is the result of the artistic search for inner spiritual essence of which all the references are merely a part. This thought represents the ultimate challenge and reward for a brush artist. The artist becomes a creator, spontaneously capturing the vitality of the brush strokes as well as the translucency of the ink and color washes. As the scenery emerges from the blank paper in front of the artist, the sensation can be compared to that of a master explorer at the first sight of a natural wonder. However, the satisfaction is much deeper, because the nature the artist discovers comes from his own mind and is his own creation.

Master landscape painter Cheng Dai-chien spent several years in the later part of his life developing the giant masterpiece, "The Great Yangtze River." The painting was done on thirty-six full-sized rice-paper sheets connected into a horizontal composition. Like most major waterways in China, the Yangtze runs eastward into the ocean. In Cheng's painting, the River turned westward. The official explanation he offered was that he was standing on the north bank watching the river. Privately, he told my father that he did not quite realize he was "fooling around" with Mother Nature until he was well underway into his major composition. Being such a humorous individual, there was no telling whether he meant it or not. To me, no explanation really was necessary.

I love the spontaneous exercises of the free-flowing imaginary sceneries. I am also a devoted student of Chinese literature, history, and geography and like to depict realistically the scenic wonders in the China I have known and loved. It is indeed a privilege to paint some of the actual scenic wonders that offer so much background in the total cultural makeup of the Chinese nation. In such cases, I do rely on my observations, feelings, and recollections, as well as photos or video films. I love to combine into one painting several scenic spots which belong to one mountain but are impossible to be viewed together in reality. I send in clouds where the factory chimneys destroy the spirit of the mountain. At times, I move mountains or temples or alter their shapes, to make them live happily together.

I do appreciate the traditional painting concepts of depicting very few reminders or traces of human existence. But China is a nation of people, and memories of all the festivities and happy times of my childhood include the happy sound of people's greetings, firecrackers, and a sea of crowds. The ancient civilization of China is symbolized by its cities, gardens, temples. It would be a great loss for artists to turn their attention totally away from people and the lives of those folks around them.

Key Concepts in Composition

Projection of Depth

Most landscape composition divides the scenery into three layers: foreground, middle ground, and background. The layers are frequently established by allowing the root area of the mountains to fade into mist.

Usually, the closer scenery is darker, more detailed, dryer, proportionally larger, and includes more diversified and warmer colors. The distant elements are lighter, less detailed, wetter, smaller, cooler and more monotone in color.

It is the root point, not the height, which determines the depth of the scenery (Figs. 18-2A, 18-2B).

Fig. 18-2 Root points determine depth

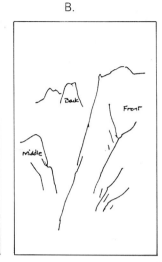

A.

B.

In order to create unity in the composition, the layers are overlapped both vertically and horizontally (Fig. 18-3A), not isolated (Fig. 18-3B).

Fig. 18-3 Overlapping

A. Mountains Overlapping

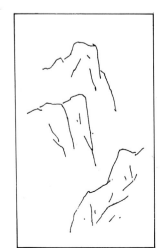

Boo-boo ⊠

B. Isolated Mountains

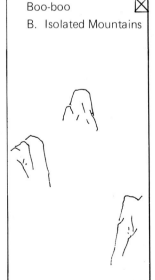

Focus

Chinese artists like to divide a composition into nine identical blocks or "jin" (井, Chinese character for well). The focus of composition is usually located in the area of the center block (Fig. 18-4).

Fig. 18-4 Focus

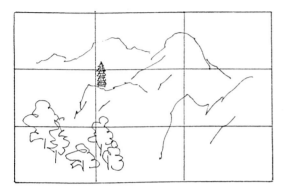

To draw attention to the focus, the steep sides of the mountains are found on the inside, allowing the mountains to greet each other. The thought is that since these mountains are stuck with each other, they really should enjoy one another's company (Fig. 18-5A), not turn away from each other (Fig. 18-5B).

Fig. 18-5 Side of mountains greeting

A. Mountains coming to center

Boo-boo Pad

B. Mountains turning away

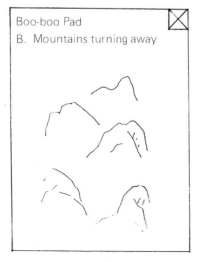

The center area and the peaks are emphasized with dark tones and more activities. As the elements move to both sides and to the baseline, they become faded and less important. Spaces are divided into "V"s to lead the viewer to the center (Fig. 18-6).

Fig. 18-6 Dark tones and V-spaces enhancing focus

Position of the Viewer

When one sees the scroll depicting the three-thousand-mile-long Yangtze River, one asks, "Where did the artist stand to view the scenery?" Most likely he stood on a boat, flowing down the river. When the emperor decided to study a long horizontal scroll of the Tai mountain range, he stood still and the scroll was rolled across in front of him, section by section, with two servants on each side doing the pulling and pushing of these mountains. Whether the viewer is moving or the scenery is moving, the idea of seeing scenery at a fixed point is not applicable.

In most cases, however, Chinese artists do adopt a fixed point for viewing their scenery. One can look up, straight ahead, or down. Taking an aerial view seems to be the preferred way of arranging a composition. In this case, the viewer's point is higher than the major portion of the scenery and the horizon is above the middle line of the painting. To compare the following pictures, Picture B typifies the Chinese viewpoint in landscape composition. There is more roof and less height to the wall, more foliage and less trunk than there is in Picture A. The viewer is able to see the surrounding plain near the house, the origin of the waterfall, and the high mountains in the distance (Figs. 18-7A, 18-7B). With this viewpoint, one can see a river with sailboats above the mountain and layer upon layer of mountains projecting into the distance. For a creative mind, this viewpoint greatly enhances the realm of the imagination.

Fig. 18-7 Comparison of Points of View

A. Low Viewpoint   B. High Viewpoint

Formation of a Flow

Organization of scenery is an enchanting process. The irregular shapes of the landscape elements require a subtle suggestion which ties all the components together and leads the viewer to travel through the whole painting and eventually stay within the focal point.

The basic ideas of (1) starting, (2) following, (3) changing, and (4) unifying (see Lesson One, The Teaching of Confucius) can serve very well in designing the overall flow of a landscape (Fig. 18-8).

The peaks of the mountains, along with their shoulder movements, passes, and waterfalls, suggest a vertical flow. The mist and river bed expand a panoramic horizontal movement. Houses, figures, bridges, and pagodas offer points of interest along the route while branches of trees direct the traffic (Figs. 18-8A, 18-8B).

Fig. 18-8 Flow in a Landscape

A. Vertical Flow

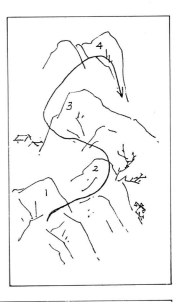

B. Horizontal Flow

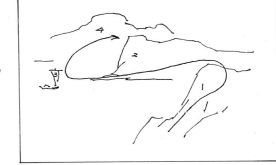

Source of Light

The positive and negative sides of mountains, trees, and structures are developed to indicate the source of light (Fig. 18-9).

However, Chinese artists usually tend to place the light source in a neutral location, directly above the scene. Judging where to put dark and light elements is based more on how to highlight the movement of the flow, or the prominence of the focal points. It is easy to explain why the dark and light do not agree with the source of light in a painting. It could be a dark-colored rock, a dark-colored leaf cluster, or the shadow of a cloud. I do this all the time and seem to be able to get away with it.

Fig. 18-9 Source of Light

Treatment of Dimension

Overlapping and crossing elements, showing different roots for different elements, along with all the points discussed earlier in the section "Projection of Depth," show the artist's concern for the overall dimensional quality of the painting. Each individual element also needs to show dimensionality.

Chinese painters are reminded by their first painting manual, **The Mustard Seed Garden Manual,** that all trees must have four arms. Derogatory perhaps, but it gives a clear picture of the need to show branches going not only left and right but also front and back. The mountain has a "nose," the brighter, protruding ridge that reaches toward us. Houses, boats, and bridges — all elements need to show three-dimensional designs (Figs. 18-10A, 18-10B, 18-10C).

Fig. 18-10 Dimensional Treatments

A. Mountains

B. Trees

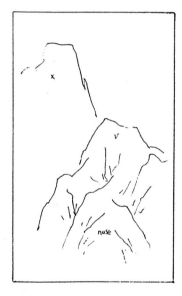
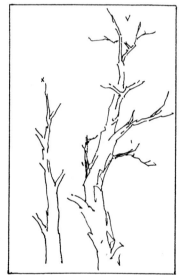

C. Structures

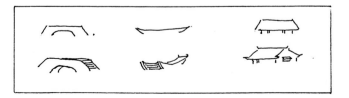

Treatment of the Border

Each scenery composition can be viewed as complete in its own right; however, it should not become isolated. Carry at least a portion of the scenery to the border to suggest continuing scenes beyond the painting and to provide a vehicle for enhancing the viewer's imagination (Fig. 18-11A).

Although scenery is shown as continuing beyond the border, Chinese artists rarely block an entire border area with solid elements. Fading or inviting mists to open some spaces have been effective ways to maintain the integrity of the borderlines. In the end, borders become hardly noticeable (Fig. 18-11B).

Fig. 18-11 Treatment of Borders

A. Extending beyond the border

B. No border blocked

A Demonstration

Preparation

Materials

Landscape painting uses different brushes and rice paper. Since this lesson is designed only to show a demonstration for students to see rather than asking students to paint, the materials for landscape painting are not included in either the Students' or the Artists' set. These materials are available through special order from OAS if needed.

Use Jen-ho or Ma (sized rice paper).

Use the Mountain Horse brush for texture, the Landscape brush for line work, the Big Idea brush for coloring, and a flat Wash brush for shading and mist.

Prepare 2 teaspoons of ink. Dilute about 1 teaspoon of ink into a medium shade and keep it in a separate dish.

Prepare a fine spray bottle filled with water (used by beauty supply shops, for instance).

Colors

In this exercise, I have tried to incorporate some of the most frequently used colors to help students identify the colors when they study the various landscape paintings in my album:

Diluted vermillion and burnt sienna for noses of mountains. Various greens mixed by blending dirty yellow and indigo for mountains, rice fields, meadows, foliage.

Many Winsor & Newton watercolors are also adopted in this exercise. I use Winsor emerald for noses of mountains, fields, meadows; manganese blue for noses of mountains, sky, and water; Winsor violet for distant mountains, mist, and sky; French ultramarine for distant mountains, clothing, and temple roofs; yellow ochre for land, buildings and structures, and mountain passes; and cerulean blue for sky and water.

The above colors are all diluted into a rather light wash so they do not conceal the work done with ink.

I also use Winsor & Newton's Pressian green mixed with charcoal gray for a dark green shade. I develop a thick mixture (dark shade) and dilute a portion into a medium strength (medium shade).

Steps

Line and Texture

Slightly dampen portions of the rice paper where the concentration of line and texture work will be (use a fine spray bottle, or a slightly dampened brush). Use light, medium, or dark ink interchangeably, or one on top of the other while the ink is still wet. Using a dry brush, with the tip split and twisted, work the texture and line from the peaks, center areas, and noses of the mountains; then lead the shoulders of the mountains down. Allow the lines and shapes to fade as they reach down into the areas intended for mist, or go to the sidelines of the paper. Add trees, structures, figures, and dots (Figs. 18-12, 18-13, 18-14).

Fig. 18-12 Line and Texture (See Page 171)

Coloring

Work the light areas (noses) first, then the shaded areas. Introduce a shaded color into each light area to integrate the whole. Allow the colors to fade according to the line and texture works. Do one mountain at a time to insure proper blending (Fig. 18-13).

Fig. 18-13 Coloring (See Page 144)

Mist

When the above procedures are completed and the painting dried, wet the whole paper. Define the mist layers along the foot of the mountains with shading and color the sky. After the painting is dried, additional dots and details are added to complete the composition (Fig. 18-14).

Fig. 18-14 Completed Landscape (See Page 144)

Lesson 19
Signature and Seals

Introduction

Using the signature, calligraphy, and seal as integral parts of composition in painting is uniquely Chinese. To authenticate and to show approval of his work, the artist uses a personal seal in red along with his signature in ink.

Your Chinese Name

I feel it is my privilege to give a Chinese name to my students to use in their masterpieces.

I usually try to choose Chinese characters which share the sound of the first names of my students. Chinese words are monosyllabic, that is, one character for one sound. Since most popular Chinese names are two-to-three characters, I tend to urge students whose names are more than three syllables to use a shortened version. For example, a name like E-li-za-be-th would be five characters. Not only is it too long to be used in a painting composition, but also it would take a whole semester just for Elizabeth to learn how to write her name.

There are more than 60,000 characters in the Chinese language, but only about 2,000 sounds. There is, therefore, a wide range of choices for selecting words which sound like and could represent your name. It really comes down to how much I like my student. So far, I have not assigned a name which has bad connotations to any of my students.

Here is a sample of the name assignment sheet I give to my students (Figs. 19-1, 19-2).

Fig. 19-1 Sample Name Assignment

Fig. 19-2 Sequence of Strokes

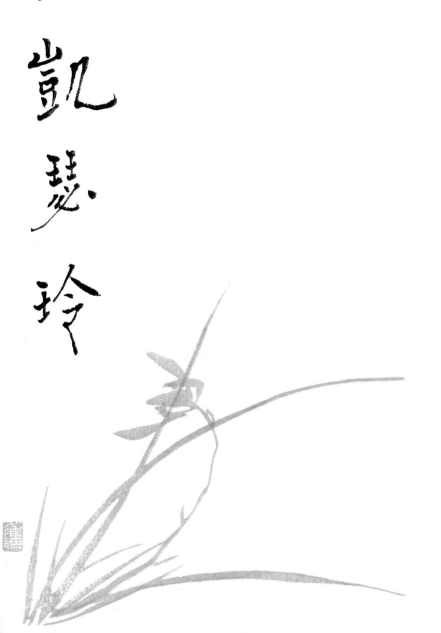

Name: Ka-th-ryn

	Sound	Meaning
(Ka)	kai	peaceful joyful balmy soothing triumphant
(th)	se	elegant bright harmony music instrument
(ryn)	ling	tinkling of jade sound of waves delicate fine

I do encourage you to also pencil-sign your painting in English and write the date in order to monitor your progress.

The signature is usually done vertically in ink. The artist may simply sign his or her name, or use his or her art name, family tradition, artistic title, academic degree, school, residence or studio, or birthplace as part of a written identification in addition to name. The year and season in which the painting is done are often included. Older artists like to include their age as part of the identification, for seniority is highly respected. A statement of purpose, or the circumstance or occasion for the painting, can also be included; for example, celebration of a birthday or farewell to a friend. Many times a title of the painting is also included in the calligraphy. Titles are usually larger than the rest of the characters. Often a poem which inspired the painting is added, or a poem might be inspired by the painting itself. The artist may invite a poet or a good calligrapher friend to compose a poem for his painting. However, the artistic ego of the artist has to allow room for the ego of his calligrapher friend. Thirty years ago, I had the opportunity to witness a horse painter who asked his calligrapher friend to render a poem to his leaping horse. The calligrapher placed the poem right in front of the horse's head; the image of the poem became a wall to halt the motion of the horse. To this day, the horse painter still refuses to talk to his calligrapher "friend."

Seals

Chinese seals are carved in two basic ways. Positive seals include seal characters which are shown in red with space around them. Negative seals include seal characters which are carved out with the space around them shown in red. The positive seal is light and airy; it represents heaven. The negative seal is more weighty and substantial; it represents earth. If the two types are the same size and used as a pair, they should be aligned vertically. The positive seal usually goes above the negative seal (Figs. 19-3A, 19-3B).

Fig. 19-3 Positive and Negative Seals

A. Positive

B. Negative

Seals can be many sizes and shapes. The square, large, and weighty ones are more commonly used at the lower corners of the painting (corner seals) (Fig. 19-4A). The rectangular, round, vertical oval-shaped, or irregular-shaped ones are used along the sides of the painting (side seals) (Fig. 19-4B).

Fig. 19-4 Different Shapes of Seals

A. Corner Seals

B. Side Seals

One seal which represents the artist is always used with the signature. This is the personal or identification seal of the artist, and often it is the artist's name seal. The artist may choose his or her full name, first or last name, or art name. Many artists use a set of identically sized seals in positive and negative types to add interest to their signature. Besides names, art names, studio, residence, or birthplace also are often used as identification seals. Most artists' identification seals are square-shaped. Since most of the time the seal script is done in a different style than the artist's signature, the image of the personal seal and signature can be totally different. Therefore, although the same characters are shown in both the signature and the seal, there is no need to worry about repetition.

The composition of the name seal with the signature can be arranged in a variety of ways. The seal can be directly below the signature to form a straight line (Fig. 19-5A). Or the seal can be placed to the lower left or right side to create a flow (Fig. 19-5B). The seal can be placed to the side of the signature to form a certain shape (Fig. 19-5C). However, it is not usually the custom to put one's name seal above one's signature.

Fig. 19-5 Signature and Personal Seal

A. Straight Line   B. Flow   C. Shape

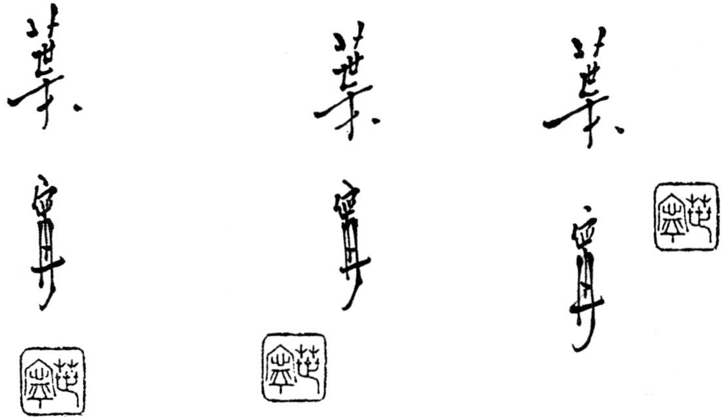

In addition to his or her signature and personal seal, the artist uses a number of other seals to enhance the composition. These seals are referred to as the side seals or mood seals; they depict the general or specific qualities of the artist, his or her works, or the virtue of the subject matter.

The meaning of mood seals can be of an infinite variety, from the sublime to the ridiculous. For example, Chi Pai-shih resented the fact that many people used his name to sell paintings and carved a seal with this message: "The world is full of art patrons who collect my works; most of them are fakes." Frustrated with his friends who requested his painting for free, artist Chen carved a seal saying, "Paper costs money." Among the seals I have ordered for my students are meanings such as "grandmother of three from Texas" and "Chinese brush painters do it with the four gentlemen." I do try to inject as much poetic quality as I can when I translate these deep thoughts into Chinese characters. Sometimes, however, I feel quite inadequate in capturing the essence of my creative American students.

In the old days, collectors were allowed to put their own seals on the paintings they acquired. The imperial courts practiced this tradition quite excessively. Some of the old paintings were blanketed by seals of the different emperors, with no respect paid to considerations of composition. Some placed their seals right at the center of the painting to show their importance. Today, such practice is generally discouraged both by artists and art patrons.

Placement of Signature and Seals

The signature calligraphy and seals are placed on the painting as an integral consideration in the overall composition.

If the painting can be divided vertically into three parts, the center part is usually left alone. The signature and seals are placed on either side to enhance the composition (Fig. 19-6).

Fig. 19-6 Three Divisions of Composition

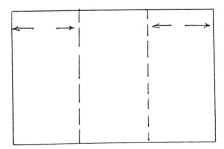

There are only two situations when the artist is about to put signature and seals on his or her painting. In the first situation, the painting is perfect — here the goal is to try not to disturb the composition with signature and seals, to make them inconspicuous, and to stay away from the key elements of the composition. In the second situation, the painting needs help — here the artist tries to use the signature and seals to strengthen the composition and to remedy its weak area.

There are several guidelines that might be helpful in determining the placement of the signature and seals.

Balancing the Weight Distribution

The most overriding concern for the placement of the signature and the seals is the balance of weight. In many cases, if the various elements of the painting are placed on a scale, the added weight of the signature and seals should balance the weight distribution of the painting (Fig. 19-7).

Fig. 19-7 Balancing Weight Distribution

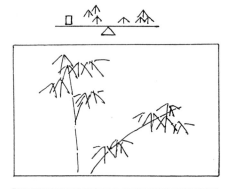

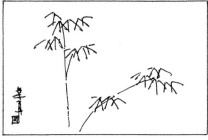

Host, Guest, and Liaison

The successful composition has a dominating host as the focal point and a supportive guest or guests as variation. The signature and seals could be used as the liaison between the two, the third element used to develop an interesting triangular shape to the composition (Figs. 19-8A, 19-8B).

If the painting already has the triangle of the host, guest, and liaison, the signature and seals could be another guest, used to construct another set of triangles with the existing guest and liaison. In this way, the signature and seals anchor the importance of the host in the middle and add a dimensional quality (Fig. 19-8C).

Fig. 19-8 Host, Guest, and Liaison

A.

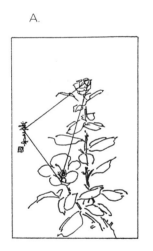

B.

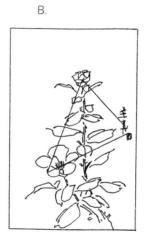

C.

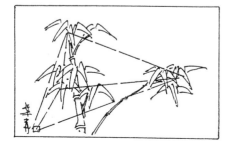

Do not align the signature and seal vertically or horizontally with the major elements of the painting. Try not to position them to compete with the host or guest (Figs. 19-9A, 19-9B, 19-9C).

Fig. 19-9 Avoid aligning with major elements

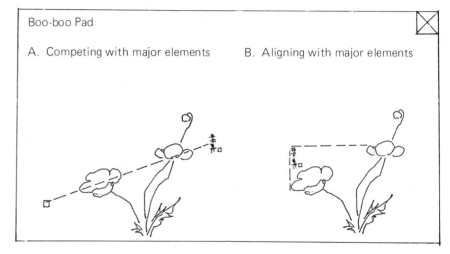

Boo-boo Pad

A. Competing with major elements   B. Aligning with major elements

C. The Correct Position

If the host and guest definitions are weak in the painting, the signature and seals can be placed near the host to strengthen the host (Fig. 19-10).

Fig. 19-10 Strengthening the host

Flow or Tendency

A successful composition creates a pleasant traveling experience for the viewer, leading the viewer to enter the painting, travel to different vista points, and eventually return to the focal point. Such a flow should not be blocked or countered by the placement of the signature and seal (Fig. 19-11A). On the other hand, if the main tendency of the painting is vague, monotonous, or broken, the properly placed signature and seals could enhance (Fig. 19-11B), add interest (Fig. 19-11C), or connect the flow (Fig. 19-11D).

Fig. 19-11 Signature and Flow

Boo-boo Pad   A. Blocking flow

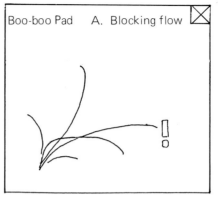

B. Enhancing flow

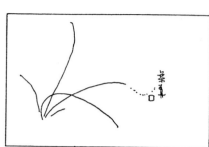

C. Adding interest to flow

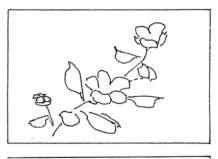

D. Connecting flow

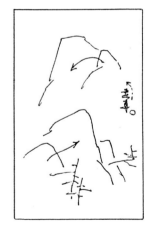

Divisions of Space

Successful placement of signature and seals expands the viewer's attention to the entire area of the painting. Spaces around the painting contribute to the overall composition. They bring the shapes of the painted subjects into focus, provide relief to the viewer, and bring a sense of freedom to the crowded areas. But spaces are not always noticeable unless certain activities are taking place within them. The use of the signature and seals serves this purpose extremely well (Figs. 19-12A, 19-12B).

In Chinese brush painting, the design of space is given the same attention as the design of painted shapes. Spaces are also shown as host and guest. If the existing spaces are well defined, the signature and seals should not alter the distribution of spaces.

Certain spaces are vital to the integrity of the painted shapes and eliminating them could ruin the design of a successful composition. Such spaces should never be used for signature or seals (Figs. 19-13A, 19-13B). Sometimes, it is even better to sign and place the seal in the painted areas rather than violate valuable spaces.

Fig. 19-13 Signature and Space

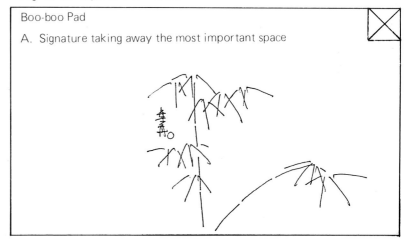

Boo-boo Pad

A. Signature taking away the most important space

Fig. 19-12 Expanding Viewer's Attention to Space

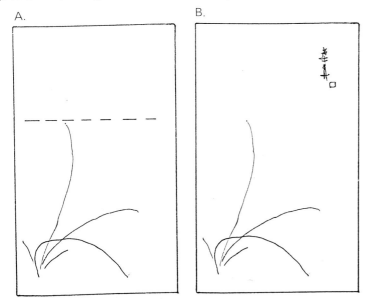

A.

B.

B. Better placement

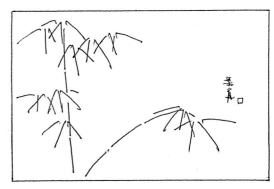

Signature and seals can also be used to reshape a monotonous space and add variation to the whole area (Fig. 19-14).

Fig. 19-14 Reshaping monotonous space

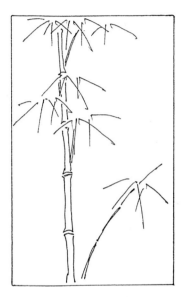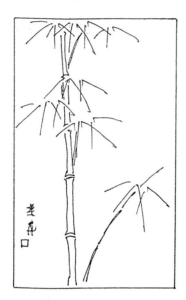

Fig. 19-15

A. Leading points create "V"

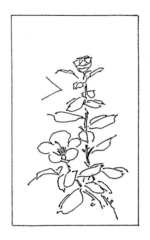

Boo-boo Pad

B. No more leading points

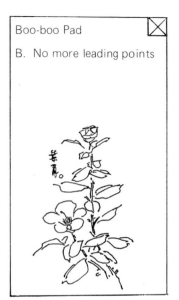

C. New "V" to lead to host flower

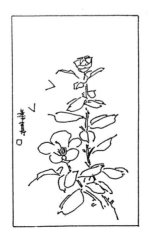

Highlighting the Shapes

Successful composition has leading points extending in various directions. These points are the spearheads of the different flows with no competitive points alongside to weaken their importance. Successfully arranged, they can divide the spaces into a series of V-shapes which converge at the focal area of the painting (Fig. 19-15A). When they are well arranged, the signature and seals should not weaken the importance of the leading points (Fig. 19-15B). If these points need help, the use of signature and seals can serve to establish new highlights to extend the painted shapes (Fig. 19-15C).

Lesson 20
Chinese Mounting

Introduction

Many students are delightfully surprised at how beautifully their paintings turn out after mounting. Mounting is a process not only for protecting the fragile rice paper, but also for smoothing all the wrinkles and bringing back all the shine and variation of the colors. It improves the visual appearance of the paintings tenfold.

Most well-known mounting studios in China have their own trade secrets. The mounting process involves backing, pasting border strips, inserting rollers, adding handles and ribbons, mending damaged areas, and doing overall restoration. Through the years, many mounting patterns and designs have developed, offering a great variety of shapes and sizes to the finished painting. Mounting is truly an outstanding art form which stands on its own merit. However, it is also interesting to note that few studios carry guarantees. Even the mounting masters freely admit things might not always go right!

During my high school days, I spent two hot summer vacations as an apprentice in Madame Kuo's studio. Madame Kuo was a sweet-faced, short, energetic lady who was a master mounting specialist. Intuitively, I sensed that there was some understanding between my mother and Madame Kuo, something to do with Madame Kuo's beautiful daughter and me, and that these experiences would help me to build character and allow me to spend time with the lovely young lady. Although reluctant, I was persuaded to move into Madame Kuo's studio.

Taiwan's summer is hot and humid. In order to prevent the paintings from being exposed to the sun or the rain, the mounting studio had no windows. To hasten the process of drying, the four corners of the room had ovens to heat up the room temperature. There were large, lacquer-coated flat tables in rows in the studio. People worked, ate, and slept in this room. As an apprentice, one did not get paid; however, one did get to do all the work and to learn all the secrets. And there was a lot to learn. In addition to mounting, I learned the Cantonese stir-frying technique, since the apprentices took turns cooking. One learned to cook well to ease the temper of those able mounting specialists who supervised the apprentices' work. This apprenticeship proved invaluable in my career development in the United States. At the time, however, it was two long, hot summers and, to my ultimate dismay, the lovely young lady went to camp both summers — I never did get to spend time with her!

Equipment and Supplies for Mounting

Finished Paintings

First of all, for mounting you need some masterpieces. There is no doubt in my mind that you must have a roomful of paintings for your first "one-person show" by now.

I usually add the signature in ink before I mount my paintings and add the seals after the paintings have been mounted. Paintings must be thoroughly dried before mounting; I usually allow a day or at least an hour to dry paintings. If you are in a hurry, a blow dryer can be used to dry them.

Acrylic Spray

If the painting is done with several colors, I usually spray it with an acrylic coating before mounting. This helps to prevent the colors from running and to bring back their intensity. Any krylon type of spray used for watercolor will do. However, do test the spray on the rice paper to see if it causes any yellowing of the paper before you use it on your paintings. I use the Artist Crystal Clear Acrylic Spray by Pictor.

Mounting Papers

Special mounting papers can be ordered through mail; or use the lighter-weight watercolor paper.

Mounting Table

A large formica-top folding table is ideal, but a plastic card table, kitchen countertop, smooth linoleum floor, or any smooth and durable surface can be used for mounting purposes. If no existing surfaces are available, cut a piece of smooth vinyl flooring or a piece of plywood for your work area.

Mounting Board

Plywood is the best material for a mounting board. It is advisable to get a large sheet (about 3' x 4') so you can mount several paintings. The board can be used on both sides and should be at least 3/8" to 1/2" thick to avoid bending.

I remember when I completed my apprenticeship at Madame Kuo's studio and returned home, I could not wait to get the mounting board that night. But I was itching to mount my own paintings to give a wonderful surprise to my mother. I figured I could paste my painting on my mother's new vinyl kitchen floor and gently peel the dried painting off the floor before my mother woke up in the morning. About 2 a.m. I heard a loud, tearing noise. I rushed into the kitchen and was stunned by the sight. My large painting, while drying and shrinking, had lifted both sides of the kitchen floor.

Paste

I usually use Metylan Cellulose wallpaper paste (or Pritt Art Paste) made by Ross/Henkel Company. It comes in a yellow box in powder form. I use a ratio of 1 part of paste power to 24 parts of cold water. To mix an appropriate amount, fill a plastic container with 3 cups of cold water and gently pour 1/8 cup of powder into the water while stirring (with a chopstick of course, or the equivalent). The powder dissolves readily in the water. Wait for two minutes, stirring occasionally. The mixture should look like loose jello or raw egg whites. If the mixture is too watery, add more powder. If it becomes too solid, add more water. When the paste is ready, pour it into a pie pan or a casserole dish so it will easily accommodate the applicator.

Traditionally, the Chinese used flour paste for mounting. This involved mixing flour with cold water and cooking the mixture over a gentle fire, vigorously stirring until it reached the boiling point. A couple of drops of liquid alum were then added to protect the paste from insects.

When I started teaching in the United States, I offered this traditional method of paste making. During one summer session, a student who was eager to mount his paintings made a glass jar full of flour paste and kept it in his car for a week. When I decided to demonstrate the mounting technique, he volunteered his paste. The whole class gathered around me. Just as I started to turn the cap to open the jar, the glass jar exploded, and the indescribably bad-smelling paste splattered, along with hundreds of shattered pieces of glass, on everyone in the classroom. To this day, this incident remains one of the worst accidents in my years of teaching. I abandoned flour paste without a second thought.

Paste Applicator

I have found the wallpaper applicator with a soft cushion base and a styrofoam handle (Fig. 20-1) very handy for mounting paintings. Usually, I cut it in half (or use two thirds) so that it is easier to apply paste and exert even pressure. If one cannot find this type of applicator, a regular 3"-wide paintbrush can be used.

Rags

You will need at least two absorbent, lint-free rags: one wet, to wipe the excess paste off the table; one dry, to dry the table. The dry rag can also be used as a presser to secure the backing paper onto the painting. Towels and diapers are very good materials for mounting rags.

Presser

The presser is an optional piece of equipment. It is used to press the back of the mounting paper after it is pasted onto the painting, to iron out wrinkles, and to squeeze off the excess paste. A bathtub scrubber is ideal. I use a scrubber manufactured by 3M Company which has a very impressive name: "Out-Scrubs-a-Scrub-Brush-Scrubber" (Fig. 20-1). It has a flat, firm cushion and a sturdy handle. It is a good product with a very bad name (How can a Chinese pronounce such a name?) If one cannot find this equipment, fold a towel several times and, grabbing it firmly, use it as a cushion and press with your hand.

A Pair of Scissors

An X-Acto Knife

A Tape Measure

(See Fig. 20-1.)

Fig. 20-1 Mounting Equipment

Mounting Procedure

Preparation

Set the mounting board vertically next to the mounting table. Be sure that all the other materials are conveniently nearby.

Clean the table and board thoroughly. Due to repeated usage, the mounting board may have strips of mounting paper left from previous mountings. You do not have to take these strips off the board; just peeling off the loose strips will be sufficient. Who knows, when you become famous, people might consider this board an "impressionistic" painting.

Cut the mounting paper with about a 2-inch margin on each side in relation to the finished painting. For example, if the painting is 16" x 24", the mounting paper should be 20" x 28". If the mounting paper comes in a roll, use a spray bottle and gently spray the mounting paper after it is cut to size to flatten it.

Place the finished painting on the mounting table face down, with its backside up. Place the painting horizontally, so that the longer side is aligned with the edge of the table in front of you. Allow a margin of about 3 inches between the edge of the table and the painting (Fig. 20-2).

Applying Paste to the Back of Painting

Apply a generous amount of paste to the applicator or paintbrush. Using your left hand to hold down the left side of the painting, start about 10 inches away from the right side and move the applicator outward to the right. Make sure each stroke goes off the painting before you return to apply the next stroke. It is easier to tilt the applicator or the brush so that only the edge is in contact with the painting (Fig. 20-2). Overlap the strokes, radiating to the topside, then the lower side, of the first stroke until the entire right side is covered with paste. Then move the stroke in the opposite direction of the first stroke, again in about a 10-inch radius, spreading the paste gradually to the left and eventually on the entire back of the painting.

Fig. 20-2 Applying Paste with Painting Facing Down

Either too little or too much paste can do harm to the mounting effort. For the first coating you should generously apply the paste everywhere, as anyplace left unglued will cause an air bubble and leave the painting with wrinkles. But too much paste in one area will delay the drying of that area and cause the painting to crack. After completing the paste coating, then, it is essential to scrape the paste off the applicator and use the applicator to go over the back of the painting again to even the paste and to remove any excess.

Wrinkles might appear during the application of the paste. If the wrinkle is a large fold, smooth it with the applicator. A small fold can be ignored, as it will be ironed out during the pressing phase of mounting.

Examine the surface closely to see if any foreign materials, such as hair or lumps of paste, are caught in the paste. Gently remove these materials.

Applying the Mounting Paper

It is now time to place the mounting paper over the painting. Since one does not see the painting below, it is important to use the table edge as a general guide to align the mounting paper. To assure the 2-inch margin, place the mounting paper about 1 inch away from the edge of the table. First land the right side of the mounting paper onto the painting and smooth it with your hand. Then gently settle the other side down onto the pasted back of the painting. Make sure the extra edges of the mounting paper stay even on all four sides (Fig. 20-3). With a wet rag, wipe off the excess paste on the table around the mounting paper.

Fig. 20-3 Aligning the Mounting Paper

Using the presser, exert pressure from the center of the backing paper outward. Make sure each stroke goes completely off the paper. This procedure firmly attaches the mounting paper to the painting, irons out wrinkles, and gets rid of excess paste. Hold the presser vertically and move from one side to the other, then hold it horizontally and move from top to bottom. Move rapidly and exert a significant amount of pressure until the mounting paper is smooth and flat (Fig. 20-4). If the mounting paper becomes uneven due to wetness, ignore it as long as you are sure that the two papers are firmly attached to each other. This temporary unevenness should disappear when the paper gets dryer.

Fig. 20-4 Pressing the Mounting Paper

Pasting the Side Strips

You should be able to tell from the back of the mounting paper where the painting borders are and identify the extra strips of the mounting paper which extend beyond the painting.

Apply a generous amount of paste to the four border strips of the mounting paper. Make sure the paste only covers the strip area beyond the painting; it is advisable to leave at least a 1/8-inch gap between the pasted area and the border of the painting. Reinforce the paste several times and make sure the four borders are thoroughly coated with ample paste (Fig. 20-5).

Fig. 20-5 Applying Paste to Border Strips

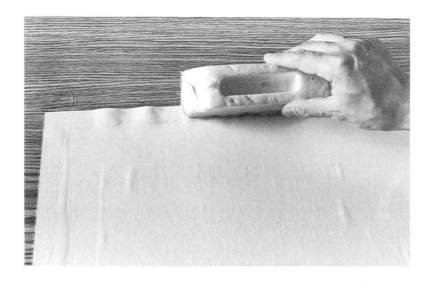

Using the Mounting Board

Lift one corner of the backing (mounting) paper to examine whether the painting is attached. If it is not, tooooo bad! Try hard to pick it up and make sure it is firmly attached. Then gently take two corners of the paper and lift the painting off the table (Fig. 20-6).

Fig. 20-6 Lifting Painting from Mounting Table

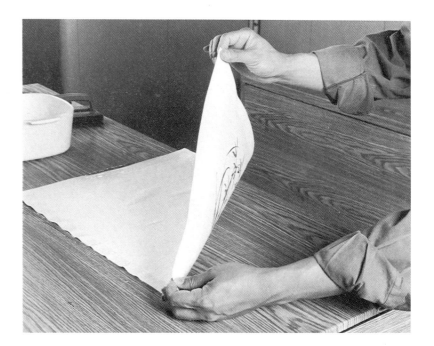

Attach the painting to the mounting board. Press along the extra side strips of the mounting paper to make sure the four sides will be firmly glued onto the mounting board. Never touch the wet surface of the painting. Should one side become unglued, cut an extra mounting paper strip and paste it onto the loose area to secure the loose side (Fig. 20-7).

Fig. 20-7 Attaching Painting to Mounting Board

Clean the mounting table with a wet rag and dry it with a dry rag to get ready for another mounting exercise.

Completing Mounting

Allow the painting to stay on the mounting board for at least 12 hours, preferably 24 hours.

When the painting is thoroughly dry, use the X-Acto knife to cut along the edge of the painting, preferably 1/8'' away from the actual border. When all sides have been cut, the painting should come off. If certain areas are still glued to the board, use a serving knife and insert it through the back of the painting to loosen it (Fig. 20-8).

Fig. 20-8 Removing Painting from Mounting Board

Finally, put the painting under a matte — or complementing border — and put the seals on to complete your masterpiece.

Materials and Supplies — Ordering Information

Please use the order forms in the back of this book to order either the **Artists' Set** or the **Students' Set** as soon as possible. These materials are carefully described in Lesson One in this guide.

An optional purchase which will greatly enrich your experience in **Chinese Brush Painting** is Ning Yeh's art album, *An Album of Chinese Brush Painting: Eighty Paintings and Ideas.* The 10¼" x 10¼", 184-page, hardcover album contains more than eighty full-page, full-color recent artworks of Ning Yeh. Each painting is accompanied by an engaging story which reveals the spiritual background of the subject as well as the personal experiences of the artist. The materials used in each painting are listed. An intriguing assortment of mood seals and a commentary on their raison d'etre, meaning, and usage are offered. This book is the resource book for the television series.

A personalized Signature and Seal Package is available, with your name's characters selected and designed by Ning Yeh, to be used as an integral part of your painting, as described in Lesson nineteen. The package includes:

A. A card which contains your name done in Chinese calligraphy on rice paper, with its meaning explained, and the sequence of each character illustrated; and

B. A stone seal with elegant carving of your name characters in ancient seal style, done by the finest sculptor in China; comes with a beautiful silk case and a red oil seal pad.

All the materials used in this instructional guide are available. For further information, please write to OAS, 10181 Crailet Drive, Huntington Beach, California 92646.

☆☆☆☆☆☆☆☆☆☆☆☆☆☆☆☆☆☆☆

發 行 者：美國加州海洋線大學
出 版 者：金絲年華股份有限公司
台北代理：欣佑股份有限公司
　　　　　台北市忠孝東路四段54號５Ｆ
　　　　　電話：(02)721-7342
印 刷 者：克帆彩色印刷製版有限公司
　　　　　台北縣三重市力行路二段28號２Ｆ

☆☆☆☆☆☆☆☆☆☆☆☆☆☆☆☆☆☆☆